DEDICATED TO

**MY FATHER AND MOTHER
AND MARTHA**

Acknowledgments

A great many people have helped me in the writing of this book. Over the years the lectures and books of Kenneth Scott Latourette have influenced my thinking about the mission of the church more than those of any other one person. I am also indebted to many members of the Drew University faculty—Will Herberg, Gordon Harland, Carl Michalson, Howard Kee, and Robert Funk—who were kind enough to guide me through an initial draft. A few of my friendly critics were known to me. My father was one. Eugene L. Smith, general secretary of the Division of World Missions was another. Fred Oden, my next door neighbor and a management consultant, and Coleman Ives, a personnel executive, were others. These four gave freely of their time and energy to help me.

I owe a special debt of gratitude to Sarah Parrott who read carefully the entire manuscript, giving special attention to its editorial needs. I want also to thank many members of the staff of the Board of Missions, Henry Sprinkle, John Wilkins, William Reid, and the typists whose counsel, encouragement, and work made my task easier.

This book was written in a relatively short period of time. This meant that my family, as well as myself, had to give it priority. Therefore, a word of thanks to Martha, my wife, Judy, Tracey, and Deborah for their patience. It was in a real sense a family project.

Acknowledgment is also given to *Time,* Harper and Row, Princeton University Press, Doubleday and Company, Oxford University Press, University of Chicago Press, The Bobbs-Merrill Company, Syracuse University Press, National Methodist Student Movement, Association Press, Friendship Press, Seabury Press, SCM Press Ltd., Abingdon Press, Alfred A. Knopf, Charles Scribner's Sons, Grove Press, The Westminster Press, Houghton Mifflin Company, P. J. Kenedy and Son, Public Affairs Press, and *Christianity and Crisis,* whose kind permission allowed quotations from the books and magazine articles mentioned in the text or appended notes.

T. K. J., Jr.

Table of Contents

Introduction 7

PART ONE

The Beginning of a New Age

1. One Missionary Era Ends 17

2. A World Civilization Emerges 31

3. The Church on the Defensive 41

PART TWO

To Whom Shall We Turn?

4. God Is a Missionary God 57

5. Faith Means Witness 69

6. The Church as a Summons to a New Humanity 83

7. The Kingdom of God Is Present and Coming 93

PART THREE

The Task of Every Christian

8. The Mission Field: A No-Man's Land between
   Faith and Unbelief 107

9. The Missionary: All Must Go, Some Are Sent 113

10. The Liberator: Every Church a Servant 127

11. The Explorer: The Churches Regroup for Expedition 139

A Postscript on Hope 149

Index 157

Introduction

THROUGHOUT the world the mood in the churches is one of search and prayer that there will be among Christians a renewal of faith. All are aware of dangers ahead. As one writer has put it, "The sky above us is dark, and this small circle of light barely enables us to see where to place our feet for the next step."[1] From every land come warnings that Christian churches are moving into a period which will test their courage. The nature of the challenges cannot be predicted in specific terms, but they are imminent. It is important, therefore, for Christians to reflect on the meaning of their Christian faith and its implications for the Church and for the world.

This book is a study book. Its primary objective is to involve the reader in the complex and critical issues facing Christian churches in the United States and throughout the world. For a few readers some of the issues will be unfamiliar, at times perhaps disquieting. For others much of the book may be familiar ground. The book does not claim to have any final word on the mission of the Church for our day. The author can only share what seem to him the significant problems and creative opportunities facing Christians. Strain as we do, none of us can see very far into the mist that covers the road ahead. Yet it is the responsibility of us all to see as much as we can and then to share with one another what we *have* seen.

In order to do this we must examine with some care the religious situation in the world today and particularly in the United States. In his book, *The Affluent Society,* John Galbraith writes that one of the most perplexing problems in a day of change is how to break through the conventional wisdom of the past. Galbraith describes the conventional wisdom of the past as a raft around which swimmers play.[2] They are reluctant to swim too far away from what has become for them their source of security.

We all know that there is truth in this. It *does* give us a feeling of

---

[1] William Hamilton, *The New Essence of Christianity* (New York: Association Press, 1961), p. 25. Copyright 1961 by National Board of Young Men's Christian Associations. Quoting Ignazio Silone.

[2] John Kenneth Galbraith, *The Affluent Society* (Boston: Houghton Mifflin Company, 1958), pp. 8-9. Copyright 1958 by John Kenneth Galbraith.

security to say what pleases others. When they nod in agreement, we forget whatever doubt we may have had as to the validity of our thought. Furthermore, we derive satisfaction from winning new people into the inner world of ideas to which we belong. Yet we know that in a time of change this can be irresponsible. Whether or not we like change, we must keep abreast of it. As we have looked beyond our own American borders, our traditional understanding of the Chinese as a passive, innocuous, happy-go-lucky people has been shattered by the rise of a highly organized, militant Chinese Communist state. As we have looked within this nation, our attitudes regarding social security, isolationism, and a Roman Catholic President have been similarly changed.

It is, therefore, natural for us to ask whether or not there has developed what we might call a "conventional wisdom" regarding the missionary movement that needs changing. Many feel that this is so. They feel, as do I, that already we are a part of an emerging new pattern of missionary work in the United States and throughout the world. Yet we are not ready for it, for we still cling to the thinking of an earlier generation. The new missionary outreach has points of similarity with the past, but in other ways it is radically different. Many knowledgeable men and women agree that one of the reasons for our present frustration, as we think of missions, is our inability to break away from the past and thereby enter fully into the possibilities of the present.

I share in this re-examination as one who was brought up in a missionary family, married the daughter of Baptist missionaries, and has been with her a missionary in both China and Malaya. Furthermore, I can think of no lifework more meaningful and important for my own children. Therefore, what I write about the "conventional missionary wisdom" of the past is written by one deeply involved in the traditional program.

This book is written with different people in mind, including especially the lay people in our churches who now support—and want to carry on intelligently—the mission of the Church to the world. The theological sections may be difficult for some. However, I have tried to write as simply as I can. The book includes these sections on theology, for the theological issues are the most critical ones we face.

This book also has in mind the *perplexed* Christians. Some are honest skeptics. When they find within themselves a feeling of emptiness, as if God had withdrawn from their lives, they see no alternative but to admit it. When they pray, they know they are saying the right words. Yet so often the words appear to be meaningless. When this happens, they are honest and say so. As they read the Scripture, they find it hard to affirm with integrity that they expect God to say something to them. If such people are reading this book, I hope they will feel that it is an honest attempt to get at some of the issues of faith that perplex us all.

A third group I have in mind are the critics of the missionary movement. They are probably more numerous within the churches than we would like to admit. George Santayana defines fanaticism as redoubling your effort when you have forgotten your aim. This is the impression made on some of these critics by the world-wide missionary movement today. They see what has happened in Communist China, Cuba, and the Congo. They have become disillusioned with the missionary movement. They are as critical of what has traditionally been called home missions as of foreign missions.

A fourth group are the college students. It is not true of them all, but many are trying desperately to see the relevance of the Christian faith for our day. They are aware of their craving for security and conformity, yet deep down there are signs of readiness in them to respond in sacrifice if they become convinced that church leaders are prepared to think and plan in new ways.

Finally, this study book is concerned for the hard-working minister, harassed, troubled, wanting to be loyal to the missionary concern of the Church, but resentful that the mission field is always somewhere else than where he is in his local church. Facing loneliness as he desperately tries to lead his congregation into new worlds of social, political, and theological thought, he wishes he could see more clearly the relevance of the mission of the Church to his own situation.

The Beginning of a New Age

As we begin this study we need to remember that we are living at the beginning of a new age. Part of our task is to try to understand its meaning for us. A world civilization is emerging. Its form is blurred, but its presence is felt. What is it like? What will it mean for the future political, economic, social, and religious patterns of mankind? Although the form of the emerging world-wide civilization is blurred, six changes that mark a transition from one age to another are clear. All this has come into clear focus only during the last fifteen years. Even the most inexperienced can recognize the six changes when they are pointed out.

(1) The first change is the emergence of the exciting, promising, and yet dangerous technological world. In some ways the technical socio-economic revolution of the past few years is the most revolutionary change of all. It is far deeper than the struggle between the communist and democratic world. It is a change that dwarfs all others in history. In past history there has been dramatic change, but nothing to compare with man's preparation to venture forth into outer space. On the front page of the *New York Times,* July 30, 1962, Richard Witkin tells of "Project Apollo," the American plan to put three men in a missile and rocket them to the moon within the next five years.

By the end of 1970, perhaps as early as 1967, three Americans will be rocketed on a journey that, until Sputnik I, only a few visionaries believed would ever take place.

Today, at a hundred hushed laboratories, at a hundred clattering factories and on a thousand cluttered drafting boards, the blueprints, the maps, the machines, the methods for that epochal journey are already taking shape.

The American astronauts will be journeying to the moon. It is the nation's hope that Russians will not have reached there first.

Whoever wins this race, it will be an event with no parallel in history. Not even Columbus' opening of the New World or the Wright brothers' first flight had consequences as profound as may emerge from the first lunar voyage.

Such a picture of the future leaves us breathless. It opens before us an entire new dimension of history. At the same time we cannot even be sure that anyone will be around in 1967 to carry out such an expedition. At the very moment that such plans for space are being made, there are other developments, both technological and political, that could lead to a disaster such as this world has never seen. We do not know for sure where we are. We cannot be certain where we are going. But one thing is clear: We have entered into an entirely new period of human history.

(2) The second change is the decline of the Western world from its once dominant position of cultural, political, and economic influence. By this I do not mean that the Western nations will not

10

play a major role in the future. They will. But it is quite certain that Europe and the United States can no longer dominate Asia and Africa as they have done for the past four hundred years. The greatest loss has come not in terms of their military power but in their moral prestige. Asians and Africans who once were convinced that the Western world was the civilization to imitate are now not so sure. They have seen in the so-called democratic West the rise of Nazism in Germany. The so-called moralistic West produces movies they will not permit to be shown in their theaters. In the 1930's the so-called stable West stumbled into a depression that shook the economy of the whole world. In 1914 and in 1939 the so-called Christian West spewed out two disastrous wars. The Asian and African disillusionment with the Western world's claim to moral leadership is one of the major changes of our day. The effects of this disillusionment we are only now beginning to feel.

(3) The third revolutionary change is the emergence of the independent nations of Asia and Africa. This has been one of the most remarkable periods of all history. Within eighteen years 800,000,000 individuals have gained political independence. There has been no letup in this rapid shift of political power: 1945, Korea; 1946, the Philippines; 1947, India and Pakistan; 1948, Burma and Ceylon; 1949, Indonesia; and during the 1950's over 26 countries in Africa alone. In the 1960's already four more African states have been formed. In 1945 seven eighths of all Muslims lived under colonial rule; today almost every Muslim lives in an independent nation. One can see immediately what this change might mean for the churches in Muslim lands.

(4) A fourth change has been the rise of the Communist states. In the past, revolutions were associated with a change of leadership at the top like a game of musical chairs. First one group and then another held the reins of power, but they all represented a traditional ruling class. This has changed. Through radical, brutal surgery the Communists have destroyed the old forms of social organization. Communism claims to be the one movement that can meet the crisis of the complex age in which we live. One third of the human race lives today in Communist societies.

(5) A fifth change is the new relationship among the world religions. A hundred years ago Christians assumed that Hinduism, Buddhism, and Islam were on the decline. Christians saw these religions as three suns setting on the horizon. In their place Chris-

11

tians were convinced that the life of Christ, like the morning sun, would continue to rise in the sky until its light covered the whole earth. Yet this is hardly the picture we see today. Today 30 per cent of the world population, or one out of three persons, are Christian. By the year 2000 the percentage will probably drop to 20 per cent, or one out of five. Hinduism, Buddhism, and Islam are on the move. Not only have all three regained their self-confidence, but also all three are making claims as world-wide religions. A reading of the Saturday edition of the *New York Times'* church page is a weekly reminder of the many Buddhist and Hindu oriented groups meeting every Sunday morning for worship in New York City. The new relationship among the great religions is another issue that deserves our study and another reminder that we are living in a new age.

(6) The final change is the emergence of a world-wide Christian Church. We sometimes forget that not only has the world changed but so also has the Church. Although it is true that the percentage of Christians is declining, it is also true that the Christian Church is the only truly world-wide religious community. Christians within these churches speak every language and wear every kind of dress. It would appear that God has been preparing the Church for just such a day as the one in which we now move.

These six revolutionary changes of our day demand the most thorough study by all Christians. Together they make it clear that the world already has moved into a new age, one entirely different from any other period of history. What are we to say about this new age? What is God doing within it? In the very midst of this turbulent and anxious time, what is God saying to Christian men and women? In a time like this it is the task of Christians to be navigators. Like the navigator of a plane flying at 40,000 feet over a continent, we must find our bearings. Where are we, and where are we going?

All navigation demands some central point of reference. For the Christian the point is Jesus Christ. He stands before us today as he stood before the disciples. For those who have eyes of faith to see, he remains the key person in our contemporary world. His presence in the Church alone explains its existence. What he says to those who hear him is as disturbing today as it was when he lived in Palestine. Like all men we want to live to ourselves; he speaks of dying for others. With all our might we struggle for personal

12

victory; he points to personal defeat as a creative way of life. As well-adjusted moderns we seek above everything else harmony; he reminds us obedience to God's will means getting into trouble. We are happiest when we associate ourselves with the beautiful; his death was ugly and harsh. We cannot help wondering why it is that we always turn back to this man when the going gets rough. But that is what we do. In our attempt to think through the mission of the Church for our day we need a deeper understanding of what it means to turn to Jesus Christ.

It would be foolish to assume that in this study book or in *any* book a final answer can be given as to the meaning of Christian faith. Always there remains a mystery about God's redemptive purpose and mission for mankind. We cannot be certain just when it began; we cannot be sure when it is going to end. We have no way to predict by any standards that the world considers reasonable that Christ will be victorious. At least we cannot prove in language acceptable to any law court that the Christian faith is better than other world religions. In the past we have tried this method of comparison in tracts, books, and sermons; but it has not been convincing either to the Hindu and Buddhist or to ourselves. Nor can we be sure just what the future of Protestantism in the United States is to be. It is under pressure from Roman Catholicism on the one hand and secularism on the other. In the final analysis we must live by faith alone

—that God has a sovereign purpose that all men should find wholeness and healing;
—that this purpose was revealed in the life, death, and resurrection of Jesus Christ;
—that the purpose is now being fulfilled in a unique way through the work of the Holy Spirit using Christian men and women within the churches.

Beyond these assurances we face many perplexing questions and difficult problems.

The questions that we will face in this study book are three. All three make sense only if they are asked from within the new age in which we live. In one sense the questions sound like the same ones asked sixty years ago. But they are not. The words are the same, but the context is so different that it is as though a great wall divided us from the world of the 19th century. The questions are these:

1. In this new age, is the Church on the defensive? Has the Church lost its way?
2. In this emerging world civilization, can man turn to himself? If not, to whom shall he turn?
3. In this time of uncertainty and change within the world-wide Church, what is the task of every Christian?

PART ONE

The Beginning of a
New Age

One
Missionary Era
Ends

"These all died in faith, not having received what was promised, but having seen it and greeted it from afar" (Hebrews 11:13).

*W*E worship a living God. It is he who is creating and re-creating our world. This has been true in the past. It is true today. The mission of God within the world does not change, but missionary eras *do* change. This is true because God moves through history, and our task in every age is to understand what it is that he wishes us to do.

From our vantage point in 1963 we can look back to the 19th century and see what happened. Before 1800 the mission of Protestantism was confined mainly to Europe. This, however, was not true of the Roman Catholic Church. From the 15th century on, there was a remarkable development of a world-wide missionary activity within the Vatican. For Protestants it was different. Three reasons are usually given why the followers of Martin Luther and John Calvin did not see the world as their responsibility.

First, it was the understanding of both Luther and Calvin that the great commission of Jesus, to "go into all the world," was meant only for Peter, James, John, and the other apostles. Second, during the 16th, 17th, and 18th centuries Protestant churches were so absorbed in consolidating their positions in areas separated from Rome that there was no energy left over for the world beyond. Finally, when the Protestants rejected the monastic orders of the Roman Church they were left without the monasteries, the traditional source of personnel for mission expansion.

However, by 1890 the situation within Protestantism had changed. There was a growing conviction that missionary concerns should include more than those close at home. It is significant to remember that John Wesley played an important part in the launching of the world-wide missionary effort. A Roman Catholic historian writes:

It was in the nineteenth century that Protestants awoke to the necessity of spreading their faith. This is not the place to account for their sudden emergence as missionary churches. Perhaps the spirit of Wesley, himself an apostle of untiring energy and faith, is at the root of this growth in missionary endeavour.[1]

This Roman Catholic's appraisal of John Wesley's influence in the world mission of the Church is not, I think, too generous. Wesley's concern for the warm heart, the enlightened mind, and the world parish certainly were significant factors.

Two missionaries whose lives can be traced to this religious awakening and who were influenced by John Wesley were Francis Asbury, who went to the colonies in North America, and William Carey, who went to India.

Francis Asbury sailed from England on September 4, 1771. He had been born into a poor family; and when he decided to go into the Methodist ministry, he was a saddler's apprentice. At the age of 26 he offered himself to John Wesley as a missionary to the colonies across the ocean. He arrived in Philadelphia on October 27, 1771. By the time of his death on March 31, 1816, the pattern of missionary work in the frontier of the United States had been determined for the Methodists, and by 1850 for other denominations as well.

William Carey was of the same generation as Francis Asbury. He was a cobbler who taught himself both Greek and Latin. His wife was illiterate when he married her. He himself taught her to read and write. While reading about the travels of Captain James Cooke and the life of David Brainerd, the young American missionary among the Indians, Carey became convinced at the age of 30 that he should go to India as a missionary.

He went not with the blessing of a large segment of even the Baptist church. Only a small minority of Christians supported him. One minister took him aside and said, "Young man, sit down. When God pleases to convert the heathen, he will do it without your aid and mine."

[1] Columba Cary-Elwes, O.S.B., *China and the Cross: A Survey of Missionary History* (New York: P. J. Kenedy & Sons, 1957), p. 211. Copyright 1957 by P. J. Kenedy & Sons.

He sailed for India in 1793. No one would have guessed that William Carey was initiating a movement into Asia that was to affect the world more profoundly than all the armies that ever marched under Napoleon.

These two men—Asbury and Carey—represented the two great missionary movements of the 19th century. One went west to America—the other went east to Asia and Africa. Both found their source of vitality among simple but devoted men and women in England and Europe. The achievements in both the West and the East were remarkable. Unquestionably one of the most amazing movements of the entire century took place on the American continent, particularly during the migration westward. Within less than a century the main stream of American life had been won to the Church.

The missionary outreach into Asia, Africa, and Latin America was successful, but in a different way. The thousands of missionaries who went into every land could not hope to see whole nations brought into the life of the Church. What they did was to establish within a century Christian communities in every corner of the earth. This came about only at great cost.

As we look at what Dr. Kenneth Scott Latourette calls this "great century" (from 1800 to 1914) we see hundreds of thousands of lives transformed by the preaching of the gospel. For literally millions there came a new understanding of God, themselves, and their world. This new understanding made possible a new world of relationships within their families and their nations. In all the history of the Church never in such a short period of time had so many new churches come to life, in so many different parts of the world, worshiping God in so many languages. What made this possible was a relatively small band of men and women whose lives were dedicated to the frontiers of that century. To think of Francis Asbury and William Carey and the thousands who followed in their footsteps is to realize that never had so few done so much for so many.

Today the Missionary Movement Is under Attack

It is amazing, then, to discover that in many parts of the world the work of men like Carey and Asbury is severely criticized. The Communists attack them as tools of colonialism. The Hindus in India and the Buddhists in Ceylon publicly accuse Indian and Ceylonese Christians as having been religious collaborators with an invading foreign religion. Much of this criticism we can put aside. However, within the criticism there are elements of truth. It is important to see the last century in clearer focus. We need to see both its strength and its weakness. The fact that we are today in a new age demands this. In the introduction to this book six changes characterizing this new situation were mentioned:

—the rise of a complex technological world, with the missile, the H-bomb, jet travel, big cities, automation, and, soon, world-wide television.
—the decline of the West from its position of dominant power.
—the emergence of the new independent nations of Asia and Africa.
—the renaissance of the classical religions.
—the threat of the Communist revolution and the totalitarian states that have grown out of it.
—the emergence of a world-wide Christian Church.

As we live in this new age, we ask: Why is it that the churches in Asia and Africa are under attack? What are the criticisms leveled by non-Christians against the churches? One way to answer these questions is to see what Christians a hundred years ago considered their missionary responsibility to be. Part of the answer lies there.

David Livingstone

In no person do we find a clearer image of that great century of work than in David Livingstone, the famous missionary to Africa. His missionary life in Africa had three main objectives. The first was to bring the light of Christ to the African people. The second was to stop the slave trade. The third was to seek out the source of the Nile River. When he died on April 27, 1873, none of these objectives had been reached. However, after his death he became a symbol of something much greater than himself. His heart was buried in the jungles of Africa near the place where he died; but his body was taken back to England and buried in Westminster Abbey. Overlooking the mighty spectacle of Victoria Falls, in Rhodesia, is a large bronze statue of Livingstone. As one studies it, one can catch the vigor of the man. He walks with a long stride toward the mission field. On his back is a pack, and in his hand a Bible. There is in his face determination, strength, courage, and stubbornness. Around the base of the statue are the words:

MISSIONARY, LIBERATOR, EXPLORER.

As we look back into that century of missionary expansion, we need to examine four words: the mission field, the missionary, the liberator, the explorer. These are words that gave direction and meaning to the last century of missionary effort. I believe that an examination of these four terms will help us understand not only the past but also ourselves.

(1) The Mission Field

When, in the late 1830's, Robert Moffat challenged Livingstone to go to Africa as a missionary, he made the mission field unforgettably clear. He described it to Livingstone as a thousand villages lost in the great reaches of Africa where smoke slowly curled its way skyward each morning, but where Christ's name had never been heard. This symbol of the mission field was meaningful for Francis Asbury as well. During his missionary career in our own country he saw the "road west" as a narrow path across mountains and rivers; but always at the end of the road, or beside it, were clusters of farmhouses from whence in the early morning smoke rose to the sky. Fifty years later the symbol had meaning for Peter Cartwright, the famous Methodist circuit rider. The mission field was a rural world; a passive, waiting world where Christ's gospel had never been heard.

This, as we can even sense today, was a powerful, persuasive, emotionally charged dramatization of a human situation. It was Biblically accurate, for it spoke of a world that was lost, alienated, separated from Jesus Christ. It was historically relevant, for the picture painted was consistent with the actual facts of the situation. Other forces, of course, were at work both in the United States and also throughout the world. The Industrial Revolution had started. The migration west was underway. Ships of many flags were on the high seas looking for trade and, behind them, competing European nations seeking world power. These factors played their part in the lives of missionaries, but by themselves they can never explain why missionaries left their homes to cross mountains and seas to make Christ known. In their minds were

21

clear pictures as to where one would find a mission field. One of many races might be living there, but the physical setting was always rural, quiet, passive, and waiting. Today this image of the mission field is not dead. It is very much alive. That is part of our problem. It still determines much of our mission thinking. But the rushing events of history have shattered this quiet rural world; the difficulty is that we have not been able to free ourselves from this mental picture so meaningful and relevant a hundred years ago, but inadequate today. We have one of three alternatives: we can forget the whole business of missionary conviction; we can try to find the few isolated places in the world where the symbol fits; or we can try in new ways to recognize a mission field when we see one in the year 1963.

(2) The Missionary

At Victoria Falls the first word under Livingstone's statue is MISSIONARY. By the end of the 19th century it was no problem to recognize a missionary. The image did not develop quickly, but when it was full grown, it was distinct. A journalist might ridicule and caricature a missionary. This was possible simply because everyone knew who he was. The distinctive characteristics were four.

The first was that of a person set apart for a higher calling of Christian discipleship, one whose vocation was above that of the minister or layman. This position of honor was not assumed by the missionaries themselves. Rather it was conferred by Christians who never went to the frontiers, as they watched the courage, devotion, and resourcefulness of those who *did* go.

A second distinguishing mark was the color of the missionary's skin. It was white. This has become so much a part of the "conventional wisdom" of the Church that Asian and African Christians find it difficult even today to call anyone a missionary who is not white.

A missionary's third distinguishing mark was that he was sent to a distant, uncivilized land. The missionary was the man who left the security of a "Christian civilization" and lived far away from culture and refinement. His post did not have to be out of the country, but it had to be beyond "civilization." The jokes in *The New Yorker* to this day, lampooning missionaries, have

22

them in some distant cannibal's cooking pot, still wearing their pith helmets.

Finally, the missionary's mark was that of a soul-winner. John Wesley's words were the measuring stick to minister and missionary alike: "You have nothing to do but save souls." When, for example, seventy-five years ago a China missionary on furlough described a coolie falling off a boat into the Yangtze River, every Christian listener saw a lost soul going to the bottom of the river without having accepted Jesus Christ. The clue to missionary preaching on the American frontier was the same. Peter Cartwright expressed it in these words:

A Methodist preacher in those days, when he felt that God had called him to preach, instead of hunting up a college or Biblical institute, hunted up a hardy pony of a horse, some travelling apparatus, and with his library always at hand, namely, Bible, Hymn Book and Discipline, he started, and with a text that never grew stale, he cried, "Behold the Lamb of God, that taketh away the sin of the world." [2]

By the end of the century, there was a growing social concern, but during the formative years, missionary motivation was seen almost entirely in individualistic, pietistic terms.

This understanding of the missionary as a white man, with a special calling, in a distant uncivilized land, saving souls, comes down to our day. It is lodged deep in our minds, determining the meaning of the missionary task today. When we see a layman in his back yard talking to his neighbor about his Christian life, or a college girl going into the Peace Corps, or an African doctor caring for a patient, we cannot recognize them as missionaries, for they do not fit the traditional image of what a missionary should be.

(3) The Liberator

The second word below the bronze statue of Livingstone is LIBERATOR. One cannot read the life of Livingstone without sensing his compassion for those in need. His life was dedicated to meeting the needs of the African people. The slave trade was his most bitter foe. During his lifetime he did not succeed

---

[2] H. Richard Niebuhr and Daniel D. Williams (eds.), *The Ministry in Historical Perspectives* (New York: Harper & Row, Publishers, Inc., 1956), pp. 239-240. Copyright 1956 by Harper & Row, Publishers, Inc.

in stopping it, but within a month after his death in 1873 the British Government closed the market at Zanzibar. Gradually the vile trade dried up. Anyone studying the 19th century dare not minimize the compassion and resourcefulness of missionaries in trying to meet human need. Although saving souls was their major motive, they were concerned with "release to the captives, and . . . to set at liberty those who are oppressed" (Luke 4:18). They opened schools, hospitals, and orphanages. This passionate concern to meet human need found expression in what was unquestionably the largest voluntary, non-government-supported program of social service ever seen. When a Chinese patient said of a missionary doctor, "He took my sickness into his own heart," the patient was recognizing this wellspring of human compassion that flowed through the mission stations of the world.

When we see this deep sense of compassion, we find it difficult to understand the attacks now leveled by Hindus and Buddhists on the men and women we want to help. The reason for their attack becomes more apparent when we see how closely the missionary movement of the 19th century was identified with Western civilization and Western political power. To this day there are those who understand the mission of the Church to the world as essentially a "civilizing" force. For them the text would read, "Go ye into all the world and *teach English* to every creature."

To say that missionaries were too closely identified with their own culture and national life does not mean that the Western governments were dictating the policies of the churches. In fact, a century ago the churches in their missionary outreach were more independent of government control than any time in the history of the Church. Yet there was sufficient identification to justify to some degree the charges hurled at Christians. To understand why churches in China and India are today on the defensive is to recognize this close association of the Christian faith with Western civilization.

For the past several hundred years there have been four widely held Western attitudes towards the non-Western world. These attitudes are lodged deep in the minds of Europeans and Americans. In the new age into which we are moving, it becomes increasingly important that we see them, and having seen them, dislodge them from their place of influence.

There was first the view that a non-Westerner was a *heathen to be converted.* Actually the word "heathen" is a good Biblical word meaning "those who live without God." However, the word has taken on another meaning. Asians and Africans understand the word to mean a depreciation of their culture. It indicates to them an attitude of arrogance and pride. One reason why churches in Ceylon, Burma, India, China, and elsewhere are on the defensive today is that the Church is paying the price of such a missionary attitude.

Second, there was the *Greek* view of the non-Westerner as a *barbarian to be civilized.* The very word "Hellenize" means to change to Greek ways of thought and life. This centuries-old image is lodged deep in the mind of the West. Too often church people succumb to it. At the end of the last century the editor of the *Central Christian Advocate* wrote, "The banner of the cross must lead civilization's advance." [3] His words reflected the thinking of the century. This today is thrown back into the faces of Asian and African Christians by their non-Christian neighbors. They are accused of having "sold out" to another culture and civilization. This, of course, is an emotional reaction. It may change in time, but not until Christians indicate that their attitude has changed too.

There was not only the Greek inheritance but also the *Roman,* which saw the non-Westerner as the *potential enemy to be pacified.* This too seeped into the Church's life. On the American frontier a hundred years ago it was the Indians who were to be pacified. In Burma it was the royal family that dared stand up to the British. When a British expeditionary army took Mandalay, Adoniram Judson, the first American missionary, was convinced it was an act of a merciful God. A few years later when British troops put down an African uprising, a Methodist bishop wrote, "There are times when the roar of the cannon is the voice of God." [4] Those who collect old phonograph records will remember that there is a recording of William Howard Taft's voice, with a plea for missions on one side of the record and an equally strong plea for a stronger Army and Navy on the other. [5]

The fourth Western attitude towards the non-Western world

[3] Kenneth M. MacKenzie, *The Robe and the Sword: The Methodist Church and the Rise of American Imperialism* (Washington, D.C.: Public Affairs Press, 1961), p. 16. Copyright 1961 by Public Affairs Press.
[4] *Ibid.*, p. 22.
[5] Paul A. Varg, *Missionaries, Chinese, and Diplomats: The American Protestant Missionary Movement in China, 1890-1952* (Princeton, New Jersey: Princeton University Press, 1958), p. 80. Copyright 1958 by Princeton University Press.

would be the *economic* view, which saw the non-Westerner as *energy to be exploited* in the development of a strong industrial economy. During the 19th century many Westerners rationalized their greed by arguing that it was an injustice against humanity to have unused resources in wealth such as oil, rubber, or gold and not exploit it. This rationalization justified much that was done in the name of economic progress. We simply have to face the facts that the mission of the Church during the 19th century was identified with this kind of mind. In 1881 a Methodist missionary in Mexico observed that "railroads are Protestant institutions . . . the whistle . . . will awaken the people to the realization that there exists a spiritual and intellectual power in Protestantism that can never be imparted by the mass and the confessional." [6] In 1900 a Methodist bishop addressed a General Conference, saying, "It is the missionary that is preparing the way for your cotton, . . . your lumber, . . . the output of your rolling mills." [7]

It would not be fair to the total picture to leave the impression that no good came out of the colonial pattern of government. The full story of colonialism and imperialism cannot be written now. We are still too close to it. However, when it can be looked at more objectively it will probably be seen as a movement that did as much good as evil:

—it introduced new concepts of justice and human rights;
—it established modern education and medical care;
—it prepared the foundations for an industrial society;
—it developed in some countries an efficient civil service.

This having been said, it is still true that the over-all record of imperialism was bad, and that the Church did not escape untainted. If we fail to see this, we are not prepared for the bitter attacks that fall on Asian and African Christian leaders. The image of the missionary as a liberator was, to say the least, a confused one. In China, India, Egypt, and elsewhere Christians are on the defensive and under criticism because of this identification of the Church with a Western imperialism that is now only a bitter memory.

(4) The Explorer

In some ways David Livingstone was more famous as an explorer than as a missionary or liberator. It would be impossible

---

[6] MacKenzie, *The Robe and the Sword,* pp. 14-15.
[7] *Ibid.,* p. 15.

to understand Livingstone without the word "explorer." He was obsessed with the dream of discovering the source of the Nile. He never found it. But in his travels to seek its source he moved back and forth across the African continent. It would be wrong to suggest that Livingstone's interest was purely adventure. As were the other missionaries who followed him, he was concerned primarily with people. On one trip, after months of travel, Livingstone and his small band appeared on the western coast of Africa. There by chance were British ships. The officers offered to take him by ship back to England. He refused their offer. He was afraid that his African porters would not be able alone to make the long trip home safely. Livingstone saw people. However, many in the churches had a different viewpoint. They too were concerned with people. But to promote "missions" they made up maps of the world. In all the places where there were no missionaries they used black.

The missionary task was to erase all the black sections. On the American frontier the same thing was true. The cry was "Westward ho!" This spirit was found in the circuit riders. They were in Oregon before the first immigrants arrived. They had crossed the mountains into Kentucky only ten years after Daniel Boone. During the cold weather a proverbial saying on the western frontier was, "There is nothing out today but crows and Methodist preachers!" Some have called the winning of the American West a victory of "muscular Christianity." Its drive was scriptural holiness; its vehicle, the denomination; its missionaries, the circuit riders. They could preach, travel, and fight. They were adventurers, pioneers, and explorers.

To the Church of the 19th century the entire world was an unexplored map. There were vast dark areas that had never heard the gospel, and throughout the century obedience meant crossing the last unexplored mountain range to see if there were people beyond who had never heard of Jesus Christ.

This image has persisted down to our day. But when jet travel can take one around the world in forty hours, how can the map be our challenge? We cannot think of the mission of the Church in geographical terms as our forefathers did. The distinctive circumstances of missionary life have changed. Yet in our unconscious mind there is still the image of the missionary as one who, like David Livingstone, must penetrate deep into the jungle area

27

seeking the source of the Nile or some hidden tribe. If our mission today does not fit this image, frustration follows. Liberia today is an illustration. The mission groups are moving out into the jungles looking for the people who are themselves moving into the capital city of Monrovia.

As we look back on the great century of Protestant missionary expansion, we cannot but be humbled by the resourcefulness, devotion, and sacrifice of men such as Francis Asbury, David Livingstone, Peter Cartwright, and many others. The 19th century mission to America and to the world was an amazing achievement. From the walls of our churches we see the pictures of the missionaries gazing down on us. Many of them are bewhiskered and strange-looking people. They were laughed at during their lifetime, caricatured by novelists and journalists, but they went by the thousands to the western frontier and to the far corners of the earth. They died by the hundreds, but always there were others to take their places. Their record is not an even one. They were often bigoted, at times some were disrespectful of other cultures and religions, and they never realized how deep was their identification with the Western world. Yet the important point is that they were sent and they went. In a mysterious way, God was able to use their obedience. The result of the offering has been millions of changed lives and the establishment throughout the United States and throughout the world of strong and virile Christian churches. Through it not only has a world-wide Church developed, but also new life has come into cultures and nations, the end of which is not yet in sight.

Our problem today is that we still see the mission of the Church at home and abroad through the eyes of those who lived in the 19th century. We cling to their understanding of what the words "mission field," "missionary," "liberator," and "explorer" should mean. But it is my conviction, shared by many others, that their particular understanding of those words is for the most part irrelevant for our day.

At the end of the Second World War, Winston Churchill published some of his speeches under the title, *The End of the Beginning*. He wrote that within a single war, one period of the struggle can definitely end and a new one begin without at any time a cessation of hostilities. This is the point we need to keep in mind. One missionary era has come to an end. In fact, a new missionary era already has emerged, the outline of which is only now beginning to form. It is a missionary era caught up within the new age in which all mankind has been thrust. We dare not separate these two eras too sharply, for they are both part of the same mission of Christian faith. Yet we cannot see the new, and appropriate unto ourselves the strength God promises, until we are freed from what has been for over a century the "conventional wisdom" regarding the mission field, the missionary, and the task of the Church.

We cannot predict for certain how the churches are going to respond to the challenges of the emerging world civilization. But one thing we can see clearly. The missionary movement both within the United States and throughout the world is changing. One missionary era has ended, and a new one has begun.

CHAPTER 2

A World Civilization Emerges

"Behold, I make all things new" (Revelation 21:5).

*O*N August 2, 1939, Dr. Albert Einstein signed a paper addressed to President Franklin Delano Roosevelt. Einstein wrote:

Some recent work by E. Fermi and L. Szilard, which has been communicated to me in manuscript, leads me to expect that the element uranium may be turned into a new and important source of energy in the immediate future. Certain aspects of the situation which has arisen seem to call for watchfulness and, if necessary, quick action on the part of the Administration. I believe therefore that it is my duty to bring to your attention the following facts and recommendations.

It may become possible to set up a nuclear chain reaction in a large mass of uranium, by which vast amounts of power and large quantities of new radium-like elements would be generated. Now it appears almost certain that this could be achieved in the immediate future.

This new phenomenon would also lead to the construction of bombs, and it is conceivable—though much less certain—that extremely powerful bombs of a new type may thus be constructed. A single bomb of this type, carried by boat and exploded in a port, might very well destroy the whole port together with some of the surrounding territory.[1]

This paper set in motion a chain of events. President Roosevelt appropriated $6,000 for a study of the matter. Some of the President's advisers felt that the project should be postponed till after the war. Others, fearful that the Germans might produce such a bomb, urged that we go ahead. Actually, the Germans abandoned their project, but we did not know this. The rest of the story is well known to the world.

---

[1] Robert C. Batchelder, *The Irreversible Decision 1939-1950* (Boston: Houghton Mifflin Company, 1962), p. 1. Copyright 1961 by Robert C. Batchelder.

In 1944 the first atomic blast was achieved. The Los Angeles papers reported it as the explosion of an ammunition dump. But when Robert Oppenheimer, the scientist, saw the explosion, the first thought that came to his mind was from the Bhagavad-Gita: "'I am become Death, the shatterer of worlds." [2] Within a few weeks the bomb hit Hiroshima. From that day all men have had to put away their conventional ideas about security, war, and diplomacy in order to adjust to this new fact of atomic power. The development of the atomic bomb is one way of describing the rise of a world civilization based on science and technology.

The New Age Was Not the One Expected

During the 19th century many Christians expected a new world to emerge, but they did not anticipate the role to be played by science and technology. They thought that the unifying factor would be the Christian faith. From where we stand looking back, however, we can see what happened. In a few decades the people of Asia and Africa realized that the power possessed by Westerners was not only in their ideas but also in their machines, engines, ships, factories, and railroads. As we saw in the preceding chapter, Christians assumed uncritically that Western civilization and the gospel were one. For them, Western civilization, including its science and technology, was a circle inside a larger circle which was the Christian faith.

On the other hand, the Chinese, Indians, Japanese, and more lately the Africans sensed that this was not so. They discovered that a machine would run as efficiently for a Hindu or a Buddhist as for a Christian. Also, they saw forces at work within Westerners inconsistent with a loving, gentle Christ. As they came more into contact with the Western world, they realized that they were dealing with two differing forces from the West. One was the scientific spirit and the other the Christian religion. There was no smaller circle within a larger one, but rather two parallel lines stretching from the Western world to theirs.

It was the second force—the scientific, technological influence of the West—that was to make the strongest impression upon them. Students from all parts of the world have flocked to colleges and universities in Europe and the United States. There they appropri-

2 Peter L. Berger, *The Noise of Solemn Assemblies: Christian Commitment and the Religious Establishment in America* (Garden City, New York: Doubleday & Company, Inc., 1961), p. 22. Copyright 1961 by Peter L. Berger.

ated the scientific method as their own and, returning to their own nations, adjusted what they had learned to Hindu, Buddhist, and Muslim ways of doing things. Like the mighty ocean Western science beats upon the shoreline of every land on earth. Out of it has come a world-wide technical civilization that has revolutionized the lives of all people.

The change of Asian, African, and Latin American life did not come quickly. For decades it appeared as if nothing was happening. It might be compared to the growth of an atoll island in the South Pacific. The island below the surface of the ocean slowly rises as coral, layer by layer, gathers on it. Finally the island breaks through the surface and can be seen by the naked eye. This happens only because of the slow but steady deposits that have been swept across the ocean and settled upon it. Such has been the impact of Western science and technology on the long established cultures and religions of Asia and Africa. The irony is that at the very moment they have uncritically opened themselves to this stream of new scientific ideas they have verbally at least rejected Western culture as being materialistic and unstable. This acceptance on the one hand of Western science and technology and on the other rejection of what they consider to be the inadequacies of Western civilization has made for an entirely new religious situation in which our mission today must live.

The Technological World Is the One All Men Want

It is no exaggeration to say that the world of science and technology is the new fact of our time. It has its limitations and dangers, but at the same time it has provided for mankind an entirely new world of relationships and possibilities. For good or ill this is the world in which we live. Furthermore, it is also the world in which we want to live. What Americans and Europeans assume to be a "better life" in terms of standards of living and political freedom is now assumed by all people to be their rightful expectation. The rest of the world has not yet been able to harness the machine and put it to its full use, but they have the expectation that this will be done. What we see, therefore, in the world today is men and women, young and old, black, yellow, brown, and white of every culture, nation, and religion, diving into the fast-flowing river of science and technology. They do not know any better than we whether this current will end up at Niagara Falls sweeping them over its crest or whether it will end in a beautiful lake. If we can see this picture, then we realize that we no longer are living in separate worlds as was true in the last century. Men and women throughout the world are increasingly wanting and expecting the same things—adequate public health systems, medical care when ill, safe and fast transportation, refrigerators, electric lights, radio, TV, two pairs of shoes, education for their children, social security, and adequate housing.

When we think of electric lights, public health, and schools we have no difficulty in understanding the wants and needs of other people. These things we expect for ourselves and would agree they have a right to them as well. However, there are other things that Asians, Africans, and Latin Americans seem to feel that we find it hard to understand. Their leaders and students seem to be perpetually angry. Even when we try to help them, we find that they will at times turn on us in anger.

Not All Men Have Technology—Thus Revolution

The world today seethes with revolution. These violent eruptions as we see them in Africa, Latin America, and Asia are traceable to a number of factors. One is the ferment of the Christian gospel as it has been preached throughout the world. Another is the experiments in democratic forms of government. A third is the frustration of not being able to appropriate the advantages of science and technology to the needs of people.

A new age is being born, but like the birth of a child it is coming with pain and struggle. It is not coming peacefully.

When, for example, an illiterate peasant in Africa, Latin America, or Asia comes into contact with this new civilization of science and technical culture, something happens to him.

Revolution

First, he attends a political rally and is shown a movie. In the movie he is introduced to the machine and its possibilities. He sees a factory turning out plows and bicycles. The next morning he returns to his rice field where his water buffalo waits for him. He looks at it a long time. In comparison to what he has seen the night before it is ridiculous that he must continue to rely on this animal in a day when Americans and Russians use machines. The water buffalo is discredited, and the peasant's frustration grows

34

when he sees his government unable to harness the machine to meet his simplest demands. He realizes that he lives in a technological world where the needs of human beings can be met; yet his children's needs are not met. His anger grows. He mutters against the old institutions, the incompetent leaders that seem helpless to lead him into a new day. When he learns that the rich nations are getting richer and the poor nations poorer, he not only is ripe for revolution, he becomes a revolutionary. The appeal of the Communist becomes a siren's song: "Workers of the world, unite. You have nothing to lose but your chains!" He listens not because he cares about the ideology of Communism, but because he is looking for a way out of the old world into the full possibilities of the new.

The Population Explosion

The peasant does not realize that one reason why his leaders cannot harness the machine is because there are so many new mouths to be fed every morning.

For every four persons on earth in 1950, there are today five. For every five today, in 40 years there will probably be 10. In the past half minute alone, about 90 babies will have been born into the world; only 60 persons will have died, leaving a net increase of 30, or 1 every second.[3]

Last year in China the population increase was somewhere around 15,000,000. The percentage increase in some parts of Latin America and Africa is even higher than in China. The pressure arising out of this rapid rise in the population, made possible by better public health, is one explanation of the struggle, frustration, and anger in the present world. Some have described the population rise as a time-bomb set to go off in 20 to 40 years. Today the population hovers around 3 billion. By 1980 it will be 4 billion; by the year 2000, 6.5 billion; and 50 years later, 13 billion.

Nationalism

Had this population increase come fifty years ago, the average peasant would have said that it was up to the family or tribe to take care of its own increase. If they couldn't handle it, then it was just too bad. But the peasant has come into contact not only with the machine, he has been introduced also to a new world of na-

[3] Speech by Eugene R. Black.

tionalism. In public meetings he is taught to sing his national anthem. He learns to salute the flag, to honor the war dead who died fighting for independence. Americans too often use the word hunger only to mean physical hunger. We need to broaden our definition of hunger, for the nationalism of many of the new independent nations represents a humiliated people's hunger for self-expression and self-determination.

The spirit and vehicle of nationalism made possible the independence of India, Indonesia, Nigeria, Ghana, and all the others. Furthermore, it is the national spirit that provides the disciplined energy and drive needed for industrialization. Finally, nationalism has provided an alternative to the old tribal and family patterns that have divided countries like Indonesia and India. Thus we see in Asia and Africa an uncritical readiness to accept the nation-state as the hope of a new day.

It has come as a shock to many Christians that the gospel is not the unifying factor in our present world, that what has brought men and women the world over into one stream of history is a scientific and technical culture. Yet, as we look at the world, we see men and women of all religions and cultures searching for a deeper center of meaning. All feel the need of it. They realize that no one nation, no one culture, no one race can live to itself. But what is that desired common center to be? Only a faith that is world-wide will have relevance in this emerging world civilization. The Christian faith is not the only faith that makes a universal claim. Hinduism, Buddhism, Islam, and Communism all make the same claim. The important point is: *only religions that claim to be for all men will have a hearing in the years ahead.*

The World Technological Civilization
Threatens Mankind's Existence

We are all aware of the possibilities for mankind provided by science and technology. We can thank God for them. The irony is that just at the moment that the United States and Europe are in a position fully to appropriate the advantages of the new age, there is growing disillusionment with it. All welcome the affluent society but there is no guarantee that it leads to a glorious new day. On the contrary, there is growing anxiety that we may be heading for disaster.

36

The Missile Revolution

The fantastic development of nuclear missiles has raised deep misgivings in the minds of many. As far as we know, the largest bombs now being stockpiled are the 20-megaton variety. There are, however, reports of 40-megaton and 50-megaton bombs being used experimentally. One wonders why we need the 40-megaton bomb when the 20-megaton type is 1,000 times more destructive than the one that destroyed Hiroshima, Japan, in 1945. This one bomb contains more destructive power than a 200-mile long freight train with each car loaded with TNT.

Thousands of megaton bombs have been manufactured by the United States and the Soviet Union and are primed for instant use. General John B. Medaris has stated that the amount of destructive nuclear power stockpiled in the American arsenal is more than enough to account for 20,000 pounds of TNT for every human being now alive.[4]

The destructive potential is incalcuable. A 20-megaton bomb, exploded in the air between Akron and Cleveland, could destroy both cities. Attached to missiles they can be sent anywhere in the world.

Other Dangers

The dangers of a technical culture go deeper than sheer physical destruction. They touch also man's freedom and his purpose for living. Since science and technology have a capacity for both good and evil, it is not difficult to see two immediate dangers.

The first danger is the power that technology can put into the hands of a few. In the final analysis, only four or five people will decide whether we will or will not become involved in nuclear war. It is generally recognized that in case of attack or threat of attack the decision of the President of the United States is final. In the kind of world in which we live, we have no alternative but to accept this. The Russians are in the same situation. What will this trend towards the centralization of power eventually mean for man's freedom?

A second danger is even more serious. It is what William Ernest Hocking calls the "night view" of the world. It is the view that what is important is *how* things work and *not why* they exist. This

---

[4] Norman Cousins, *In Place of Folly* (New York: Harper & Row, Publishers, Inc., 1961), p. 14. Copyright 1961 by Norman Cousins.

unwillingness to deal with questions of purpose has characterized to date the technological revolution. The harvest is already apparent in the West. T. S. Eliot writes that Western man has become like "bits of paper blown in the wind." A critical danger within this new emerging civilization is that Asians, Africans, and Latin Americans will uncritically accept science as a religion, as have many in the West. It may become for them, as it is for many Westerners, the ultimate source of truth. Already there are indications that this may happen. One can only look to history, writes Hocking, to remember that when cultures imitate each other they have a tendency to adopt perversions as readily if not more readily than the more creative possibilities. One of the challenges of the mission of the Church today is to try to head off this trend.

The Emerging World Civilization Opens a
New Opportunity for All Religions

In a world technical culture that is both a promise and a threat, the religions of the world find their challenge and opportunity. As we have noted, the other world religions have been revised. They are proclaiming their respective ways of life and truth as a deeper center of this new world society. Hinduism is serene in its confidence that the next century will rest on the basic premise that "all religions are a manifestation of the same reality." It sees Christianity, Communism, and Islam as partial and one-sided expressions of this one reality. Buddhism sees *its* way as mankind's hope for peace. When one hears Hindus, Muslims, and Buddhists making these claims about themselves, one realizes that the situation differs from that in the 19th century, when Christians had the world pretty much to themselves.

Obviously a new situation confronts Christianity. For the short run at least, the center of emerging world civilization is secular, scientific, technological. This view has provided a unifying point, but can it survive as the center?

Dr. Arnold Toynbee, playing the part of both analyst and soothsayer, projects himself into the future in order to look back and see what is happening today. He writes that historians in 2063, one hundred years from now, will say that the great event of the 20th century was the impact of Western civilization upon all other living societies of that century. Historians a thousand years later, in 3063, will interpret the 20th century primarily as the beginning of a mas-

38

sive counter-offensive of the Eastern religious ideas against Christianity. By 4063, writes Toynbee, historians will be interpreting the 20th century as that hundred-year period when mankind made his first steps toward a single global civilization. Toynbee adds that the center of that new civilization will be neither technics, economics, war, nor politics, but religion.[5]

Some Implications for Christians

In this new age in which men are being drawn together, all religions will have their opportunity to speak. In spite of advances in science, man's condition fundamentally has not changed. Men and women must still face sickness, failure, heartache, pain, and death. In spite of the technological development—indeed, because of it— men and women the world over are in deep agony of spirit, wandering in a misty land trying to make sense of their fragments of knowledge.

No one knows how successfully Hinduism, Buddhism, Islam, or Communism will cope with this emerging world technical civilization. There is also no assurance that Christians in this generation will rise to its challenge. It is important for Christians to think of their "mission to the world" in new ways. New content must be given to the words "mission field," "missionary," "liberator," and "explorer." As was pointed out in the preceding chapter, 19th century understanding is no longer adequate. Since we are living in a new age it would be tragic indeed to hold to the old just when God has thrust every Christian and every church into a new and exciting era.

In light of mankind's search for a deeper center of meaning than science can provide, it is of no small significance that all nations of the earth use the Christian calendar. Even Communists and Hindus acknowledge living in the year 1963 A.D. This calendar they have accepted for practical reasons. They give no religious significance to it. But this acceptance says something to Christians. What happened nineteen hundred and sixty-three years ago to warrant the calendars of the world being set by that particular moment? Is it to Christ that this world-wide technical civilization unwittingly points? In unconscious and involuntary ways are men and women the world over acknowledging that Jesus Christ is at the center of

[5] See Hendrik Kraemer, *World Culture and World Religions: The Coming Dialogue* (Philadelphia: The Westminster Press, 1960), p. 12. Copyright 1960 by Hendrik Kraemer.

this fantastic era into which we are moving? Christians say so. But are Christians saying so in language that can be understood? This is the missionary problem confronting every Christian within every nation.

It would be inaccurate and misleading to end this chapter suggesting that all men and women are accepting Christ as the center of the new age. They may do so later, but they are not doing so today. What unites mankind now is not religion, but a scientific and technical culture. This new culture has signs of great vigor, but in the long run it is the Christian's conviction that religion will make the difference. But which one will it be? All religions including Communism, are in the marketplace, jostling one another for position. Which of them will provide the center of the new civilization? Will the center be Buddha, Mohammed, Marx, Gandhi, or Christ? Is it to be no one of these but a synthesis of them? These are some of the questions that Christians must struggle with as they rethink their mission within an emerging world civilization.

CHAPTER 3

The Church
On the Defensive

"In the world you have tribulation; but be of good cheer, I have overcome the world" (John 16:33).

WHEN we live by faith that God is a living God, making and remaking his world, and thereby forcing us out of our conventional ways of thinking, is it any wonder that we are uneasy? The redemptive mission of God continues, and in it we live; but one missionary era has ended, and the characteristics of the new era are not immediately apparent. As we try to get our bearings, we need to look at what has happened on the one hand to American Protestants and on the other to the Chinese churches.

I do not include this chapter as an opportunity to criticize. I am weary of the endless books that seem to take delight in analyzing the weaknesses of Protestantism. As I read some of these books, I am troubled by the unconcealed satisfaction of the author when he finds a new contradiction to expose. I take no pleasure in seeing weaknesses within Protestantism. We know they are there. If there are those who say that they have not felt the cold hand of anxiety upon their lives, it is because they are looking without realism at the world in which we live.

It is immeasurably reassuring to me that in spite of a recognition that all is not well within, Protestants have been willing to take chances both in this country and abroad to strengthen what has been called traditionally the missionary outreach of the Church.

Having said this, I still consider it important to take a critical look at American and Chinese Protestantism.

Experiencing a Mild Earthquake

Some years ago in Berkeley, California, I experienced a mild earthquake. Standing in the kitchen of our small apartment, I noticed the pan on the stove shaking and the dishes on the table

41

rattled. The tremor lasted only a few moments. Within a minute all our neighbors were outside. "What has happened?" I asked. Everything seemed the same. Nothing was broken. Yet I had a feeling that the very foundations of California had been shaken.

A mild earthquake resembles, I think, the situation in which we find ourselves when we reflect on the end of a missionary era and the rise of a technological world civilization. We have not felt the impact of the last war in the same way as Europeans or Asians. Nor have we felt a weakening of our national power. On the contrary, we have never been stronger. Yet our reactions as Protestants have been like those of a person following a mild earthquake. "What has happened?" we ask. Everything seems the same. We are still strong. The nation is secure. Protestant churches are growing. But there is a feeling that the foundations have been shaken, and we would like to know what it means.

The Theological Erosion

One reason for hesitation and indecisiveness within American Protestants is its uncertainty about Christian faith. This uncertainty is partly a problem of language. In a scientific age it has become difficult to express the deepest experiences of the Christian faith in a language of the last century. Some find meaning in phrases such as "washed in the blood of Christ," but others do not. Part of the uncertainty in Protestantism is an indication that a transition in the use of language is taking place.

But there is a deeper issue than that of language. In some cases the content of the Christian faith is questioned. Faced, for example, with the question whether or not Jesus Christ is unique for all men, many Protestants hesitate. Underneath the prayers we repeat, the creeds we share, the sermons we preach, there is in many parts of the Church a questioning as to the validity of the historic teaching of the Church. If Jesus were only an exceptionally fine man and no more, the root of faith has been cut. When this happens, it is no surprise that missionary conviction is lost. Dr. James Stewart, the well-known Scottish preacher, quotes from James Denney: "Some people do not believe in missions. They have no right to believe in missions: they do not believe in Christ." [1]

This is a blunt reminder that if we talk about a mission to the

---

[1] James S. Stewart, D.D., *Thine Is the Kingdom* (New York: Charles Scribner's Sons, 1956), p. 15. Copyrighted.

world, our motivation must come out of what we have to say about Jesus Christ.

This kind of particularity goes against the grain. To many Protestants it seems intolerant, arrogant, and narrow-minded, and they are reluctant to draw so sharp a line. It is counter to the mood of many who are saying that all religions are essentially the same. It is contrary also to the conviction that what is important is not what a man believes but whether or not he is *sincere* in what he believes. We say to each other, "If you are sincere in what you believe, that is all that is important." This is partly the price of living in a nation with so many different religious points of view.

We can sympathize with former President Eisenhower when he said, "Our government makes no sense unless it is founded in a deeply religious faith—and I don't care what it is!" [2] As President he could probably say nothing else, but what does this mean, in terms of missionary motivation, to the non-Christian world?

Bishop Stephen Neill uses Nietzsche's parable of the "madman at noon" to describe the religious situation in much of the Western world. In the parable a man with a lantern ran into the market place calling out, "I seek God!" The bystanders, who were church-going people, were amused. They laughingly said, "Why? Is God lost? Has he taken a vacation? Has he emigrated?" But the man cried out again, "Where is God gone? I mean to tell you. We have killed him, you and I. We are his murderers!" [3]

Bishop Neill writes that Nietzsche was not attacking God when he wrote this parable. With cool precision, he was analyzing what was taking place in Europe at the end of the last century. Bishop Neill comments further that Nietzsche saw what others did not—the gradual fading, from the mind of Western man, of the awareness of God. Nietzsche's predictions were all too true. For evidence one has only to look at the religious situation in Germany prior to Hitler's rise to power. Whether or not this parable is relevant for the American scene only time can tell. It is, however, a parable on which every Christian should ponder.

---

[2] *New York Times* (December 23, 1952), p. 16. Quoted by Will Herberg in *Protestant-Catholic-Jew: An Essay in American Religious Sociology* (Garden City, New York: Doubleday & Company, Inc., 1955), p. 97. Copyright 1955 by Will Herberg.

[3] Stephen Neill, *Christian Faith and Other Faiths: The Christian Dialogue with Other Religions* (London: Oxford University Press, 1961), p. 191. Copyright 1961 by Oxford University Press.

The Dream of a Protestant Nation

A second explanation for Protestant frustration is the changing pattern in American religious life. Protestants in the United States are not in the same position as we were some fifty years ago. When the Revolutionary War was fought against England, 98.5 per cent of the people in this country were of Protestant stock. This does not mean that all were within Christian churches. Actually at that time only 7 per cent of the total were church members. But it does mean that they were not Roman Catholics or Jews. Their background was Protestant; and although they were unevangelized, their inheritance was within the Protestant tradition.

Throughout the nineteenth century this predominant position was maintained. One of the motives of the missionary movement to the American frontier was fear of the Roman Catholic Church. When Horace Bushnell and Lyman Beecher made their pleas for a strong missionary movement west, they presented three concerns. The first was the struggle against the "infidels." They had in mind men like Benjamin Franklin, who had been influenced by the agnosticism in France. The second concern was what they called the "barbarianism" of the West. The third concern was getting there before the Roman Catholics. Even at that time there was fear that the Roman Catholic Church would grow in power. The fear was unrealistic, for when Bushnell and Beecher wrote their pamphlets, the Roman Church numbered only a few thousand in America.

Later in the nineteenth century a marked change occurred. The immigration of millions of Roman Catholics and Jews fundamentally altered the balance in the United States. For the first fifty years of the century the Roman Catholic Church concentrated its energy on helping these new immigrants become part of their adopted homeland. Only in the last forty years has that church felt secure enough to assert itself as a legitimate part of national life.

It is no secret that in the United States today Protestants play a role very different from that in the nineteenth century. The nation has not been Protestantized, as Protestants once dreamed. In 1933 Alfred North Whitehead, a Harvard philosopher, said of Protestantism in general: "Its dogmas no longer dominate; its divisions no longer interest; its institutions no longer direct the patterns of life." [4] This statement is strong but it reflects a change.

---

[4] Winthrop S. Hudson, *American Protestantism* (Chicago: The University of Chicago Press, 1961), p. 166. Copyright 1961 by The University of Chicago Press.

In more recent days the associate editor of the *Christian Century,* Martin Marty, has written: "Whatever else it included, the 'old shape' of American religion was basically Protestant. Whatever else it includes, the 'new shape' of American religion is not basically Protestant." [5]

This does not suggest for a moment that Protestants will not remain influential and the majority of the nation. Nor does it mean that we have not made tremendous strides forward in our mission to America. We have. But the dream of a Protestant nation, an entirely new creation under God, as reflected in the hymn of Katharine Lee Bates, "O Beautiful for Spacious Skies," has not been realized. This has been hard for Protestants to take.

The Loss of Self-Confidence

A third reason for Protestant indecisiveness is a growing self-distrust and loss of self-confidence. Samuel Butler is reported to have said of the farmers of Battersby: "They would have been equally horrified to have heard the gospel of Jesus Christ doubted or seen it practiced." Christians have a growing suspicion that we have become too much like the secular world around us. Many of us have a gnawing sense of guilt that we have not lived up either to the world's expectations of us as Christians or of our own expectations. The theologian, P. T. Forsyth, once wrote: "Why the church is too little missionary is that it is established on good terms with the world instead of being a foreign mission from another."

Deep down in our bones we feel that Forsyth may be right. The American culture is *competitive,* and in many communities the race is on to see which church can get the most members. Our culture is *activistic.* Therefore, the important thing in the communal life of the church is not Bible study and small fellowship groups, but Rotary-like suppers, P.T.A.-like organizational meetings, and country club-like socials. Our society is *conformist;* therefore when the official board of a church meets to discuss a local problem on race, it first tunes in the radar-system to see what the community is thinking before making a decision as to what it should do.

Our culture is *prejudiced,* and our churches follow class lines. With 40,000,000 persons now in the suburbs, the trend toward class churches which started years ago has gained momentum. Most Prot-

[5] Martin E. Marty, *The New Shape of American Religion* (New York: Harper & Row, Publishers, Inc., 1959), p. 73. Copyright 1958, 1959 by Martin E. Marty.

45

estant churches are made up of men and women of the same social and economic group. They tend to freeze out those not identical with their interests and social standing. The holiness groups, therefore, tend to work more among the lower economic groups; the Methodists, Lutherans, Baptists, and Presbyterians among the middle class; and the Episcopalians among the wealthier groups. One need not elaborate on what this has meant in the racial situation. The facts are well known to all. As we are constantly reminded, there is no hour more segregated than 11 o'clock on Sunday morning. Our culture is *security conscious*. Therefore, when we hear of Christians in Asia or Africa who welcome revolution and change, we assume automatically that they are unreliable.

Nothing saps energy and produces self-distrust quicker than guilt. It is like a hidden, inner fire. We see the smoke, but we can't find and quench the flame. If American Protestants have become too much like the world in which we live, how can we recover missionary vitality without penitence and God's forgiveness? When confession has been made and forgiveness obtained, we will be able to forgive Christians in Communist China who have conformed too much to the Communist society in which they live.

The Complexity of Decisions

A fourth source of our problem is the complexity of the issues we face. When we recognize our Christian responsibility in political and economic affairs, we often give up simply because the decisions to be made are so complex. Numerically those affiliated with the Church represent 62 per cent of the population. The growth of the churches has been remarkable. In 1920 only 43 per cent were church members. During the Civil War it was 25 per cent. It is clear that during the past 100 years we have witnessed an amazing missionary movement in the United States. With such numerical strength one would assume that we would know just what to do to create a Christian nation. But it has not worked out that way. Christian leaders are divided in their judgment as to what is right and wrong. What should we do about disarmament? What about nuclear testing? The choices we make are not simple ones. The temptation is to retreat from the field and leave these issues for politicians to settle.

All this points up the frustration of many of us with the world in which we live. We give our wealth to help other nations, and find them not only ungrateful but actually resentful of us. We house the United Nations and pay a big share of its bills, and find that this does not provide a stable world.

When we look at these problems within Protestantism and add to them the disintegration of the missionary images of the nineteenth century, one can understand why our missionary thinking is confused.

In spite of all this, as pointed out earlier, we have not given up. During this period there has been within the Protestant churches a release of energy that has had a profound effect in many parts of the world. In other words, no matter how confused our motives or blurred the images, we learned long ago that missionary obedience does not mean that we always know exactly where we are going. We have learned that new direction comes when we are willing to take chances and try something new. Within the United States and abroad there are more missionaries today than at any time in the history of the Church. Furthermore, the giving to support this work goes up every year.

Thus we see that at the very time that the image of a missionary has become blurred, many within the churches have responded anew to missionary obedience and service. It is important that we keep this in mind. New images of what the missionary movement can be for this day will not arise simply out of discussion; they will come only out of concrete experiments. Some of these experiments, such as the "sit-in" demonstrations, will be controversial and can easily be misunderstood.

It would be a disservice to end this section without speaking again of the mild earthquake. The marching feet of history have not trampled the American world with the same ruthlessness as in Europe, Asia, and Africa; but we have felt our world shake, mild though the tremor has been. It is a reminder that we must reflect on the meaning of these events and what God is saying to us through them. Leadership for the years ahead is demanding, and all is not well in the land or in the churches. Our large church budgets and all our activity cannot in themselves bring new life to even one man unless God is in them.

The Christian life is *dependence* on God, and the Christian mission is *obedience* to God. From the earliest days of the Church's life this has been the sequence essential to renewal and recovery. First, dependence on God; then, flowing out of dependence, obedience. In a secularized age of self-sufficiency, dependence has become a difficult hurdle for us. How, then, can we discern in Scripture the relationship to God that will rekindle for us all the missionary obedience that comes out of dependence upon the living God?

The Church in Communist China

If the experience of Protestants in the United States has been of a mild earthquake, the experience of Christians in Communist China has been of a violent one. A Methodist Chinese layman who lived for ten years in Communist China recently wrote, "During such an unprecedented historical change as the one that has taken place on the Chinese mainland, we cannot expect religion to exist as before." As we consider the mission of the Church in the contemporary world, mention must be made of Christians in China.[6] For over 100 years the mission to China dominated the thinking and planning of both the Protestant and Roman churches. In the 1920's there were over 7,000 Protestant missionaries in China and an equal number of Roman Catholics. In 1937 half of all Chinese hospital beds were in the 300 Christian institutions. There were 13 Christian universities, over 1,000 high schools, and hundreds of churches. Protestants numbered 1,000,000 and Romans 2,500,000. All this has changed. With the coming of the Communists in all the provinces of China, Christian hospitals, colleges, and high schools were all taken over by the government. The missionaries have left.[7] About a third of the church membership has melted away.

The Communist Party has been determined to remake every aspect of Chinese life. The crucial word has been *tou cheng* or "struggle." No one has escaped tension and uncertainty, including the members of the Communist Party. It has been a family struggle. Sons and daughters have been encouraged to denounce their fathers and mothers as traitors worthy of death. It has been a class struggle. Groups have been pitted against each other. Literally millions perished in the land reform trials of 1951 and 1952. It has been a national struggle. Every individual or group of individuals that in any way challenged the government has been considered an enemy. It has been an international struggle, directed largely against the United States.

In all Chinese history there is nothing like it: long hours of

---

[6] *Cf.* the author's chapter, "The Mission to China" in the symposium edited by John R. Wilkins *et al.*, *The Christian Mission Today* (New York: Abingdon Press, 1960) pages 105-115.
[7] Perhaps a few missionaries, some presumed dead, remain in China, imprisoned or otherwise cut off from communication with the outside world.

work, little rest, no privacy, unceasing propaganda. The pressure on everyone, from party member to political prisoner, has been relentless. There is no question but that destructive forces have been released. This has been true of all revolutions, but perhaps in this one more than others. At the same time, as in all revolutions, there have been major achievements. The nation has been unified. The pride of the Chinese has been restored. The Communists are fully aware that their experiment is still passing through a critical state. There is no final guarantee that they will be successful. The stand-and of living remains marginal for all; and with the growing pressure of population, unless there is a near-miracle in production, the dreaded peasant discontent and unrest will return to haunt Communist rule as it did its predecessors.

It is in this restless, uncertain, constantly changing revolutionary situation that Chinese Christians have to live. Indoctrination has been overwhelming. Nerves have been rubbed raw by blaring radios, frequent mass meetings, constant intrusion by party officials or local committees. The Communists have attempted to convert Christians into what the Communists call "progressive" ways of thinking.

As we examine the record of the past fourteen years we can now see with some clarity what has happened to the Christians.

First of all they have been humbled. To their surprise Christians found themselves dealing with Communist leaders, most of them young, who were hard workers, disciplined, and self-confident. Christians soon realized that the Communists were ready to sacrifice themselves for their cause with an abandon that Christians did not feel towards theirs. They also discovered that there was an unexpected puritanical strain in the Communists. Prostitution was stamped out. The subtle forms of political corruption that had undermined so much Chinese political life were brought under control. It was a shock to the Christian to find that the Communists did what Christians for so long claimed to be their objective. In the new Communist society it was the lower classes, the workers, the peasants, the underprivileged, who were elevated to the highest position of prestige. As we now see, much of this was a hoax. Yet it is true that a new relationship has been established between the scholar and the ordinary worker. When Muriel Lester, the well-known British Christian, visited Shanghai, she had an evening meal in a restaurant with her Chinese friends. One of the men, a leading educator, did not eat all his rice. A waiter passed by and saw his half-filled bowl. He leaned over and commented, "Comrade, don't you think you had better finish your rice?" The Chinese scholar said nothing but did as he had been asked. He then turned to Miss Lester and said, "We have learned with new humility to listen to the workers." One reason for his action no doubt was fear. But there would be more to it than that. Christians have been humbled by their realization in years past that they did not identify themselves as they should have with the common people of China. This is a lesson that applies not only to China but also to every country.

Christians have been frightened. The Communist strategy has been to win over their opposition by persuasion. However, no one questions for a moment what happens to anyone who challenges the Communist Party's rule. The evidence is there to see. In the early 1950's anywhere from 1,000,000 to 5,000,000 men and women were liquidated. Since then executions have been less frequent. Nevertheless, hundreds of thousands are still in prison or in labor reform camps. We know of six Methodist ministers in Peking who were arrested and sent to prison. It is part of the record that one Methodist Bishop, W. Y. Chen, spent five years in prison. Other leaders, such as Wang Ming Tao, a courageous, outspoken, Christian evangelist, were arrested and imprisoned. In such a situation one could only expect Christians to be frightened.

Christians have experienced disgrace. The Communists charge that Christianity is a tool of American imperialism. They have relentlessly hammered away at that idea, saying that the United States entered China with a gun in one hand and a Bible in the other. The Christian Church in China is accused of having had close contacts with the United States and is therefore suspect. Many Christian leaders have been called upon publicly to attack the United States and their American friends as proof of their own loyalty to the New China. In 1952 when Bishop Carlton Lacy died in Foochow, China, only his cook was permitted to attend the funeral. On another occasion when a Chinese minister wrote on a government form that his work was that of a pastor, the Party officials changed the word to read, "a dealer in superstition." In 1950 the Communists put out a classified list of the types of workers in society. The two at the bottom were prostitutes and missionaries. The prostitute was placed one rung higher on the social ladder than the missionary.

50

They have been isolated. By 1952 most Western missionaries were gone. Since then there has been no official contact between the Christians in China and any related church bodies outside China. There have been a few delegations of Christians from Australia, Japan, India, and Europe visiting China. However, the Chinese churches have sent no delegations to meetings outside the Communist world.[8]

The churches have been weakened. Over the years regular church services, Bible study and prayer meetings, although officially permitted, have gradually been reduced. In Peking there are now four churches open for worship. In Shanghai the number is twenty-one. Fifteen years ago the number in Shanghai was over 200 and in Peking 60. One reason why laymen have been reluctant to attend church services is the feeling among some that too many pastors have knuckled under to Communist pressure. There have been few serious Christian books written. Only one periodical, *T'ien Feng* (The Heavenly Wind) is still in publication. Even in it considerable space is given to political propaganda.

Christians have been silenced. In a Communist society political neutrality is considered as dangerous as outright opposition. Everyone must publicly support the government. As one Christian has described it, it is like riding on a train. There are many cars, as there are various segments of society in China. But there is only one engine and one set of tracks. The Communist Party is the engine; the tracks are the "party line." There is no freedom to challenge either. To do so is to become "an enemy of the people." In a few cases Christians such as Wang Ming Tao have taken a stand. When they have, their days of freedom have been numbered.

They have been manipulated. There have been two serious failures of Christians in China. The first resulted from the accusation meetings. Christians did not realize that one of the techniques of a Communist seizure of power is to turn friend against friend. The accusations that sent a Methodist Bishop to prison came from his fellow-Christians, some of whom were leading Methodists. The same was true for others. It has hardly been a bright record in the Church's life.

A second serious failure has been the inability of Christian leaders to distinguish between truth and falsehood. They have participated

---

[8] Bishop K. H. Ting in 1958 did attend the Lambeth Conference in England. However, this was not an official delegation.

in campaigns of vilification against each other and against sister churches that have no substance in fact. For example, one Christian leader was sent to prison. The church press stated that there was indisputable evidence that the charges were true. A few months later the government released the man, publicly acknowledging that the accusations were false. This left the Christians who edited the church press in a difficult position. Those of us who live outside of China are in no position to judge our Chinese friends. We need to see what they are going through so that we will not make the same mistakes ourselves.

There is no question but that Christians in China have faced hardship and suffering during these past fourteen years. All have been on the defensive. The miracle is that Christians by the tens of thousands have remained faithful. *In fact, they are confident that the Christian churches will not only survive but also will grow.* As late as 1961, 319 Christian leaders gathered in a National Christian Conference in Shanghai. There were, of course, political overtones in the conference. But this should not take our eyes off the central fact that there are men and women still claiming that Jesus Christ is to be the final center of China's life.

In order to survive, Christians have had to work out a *modus vivendi* with the Communist Party. It is true that Christians have made mistakes. In times of testing many have lost their courage. But he who is without sin can cast the first stone! The significant point is that they still have the courage to acknowledge publicly their Christian faith.

What Christians in China have experienced has taught us three lessons:

First, self-support is essential for every church. In the past the financial dependence of the Chinese churches on Western support was too great. This is a lesson other churches in Asia and Africa need to keep in mind.

Second, the selection and training of the ministry is important. There is an old Chinese saying, "In severe winter you will know the endurance of the pine and cypress trees; in times of chaos loyal ministers will be manifested." Some pastors have not met the test.

Third, the greatest lesson is that *even in a Communist society Christian churches can survive and witness.* Christians can continue to do God's will. Where this obedience exists, God can use it in fulfilling his purposes.

To Sum Up

It is obvious that we live in a day very different from the 19th century. We can see the effects of this new age on American Protestantism and the churches in China. For both the foundations have shaken. For Americans it has been a mild earthquake, for Chinese Christians a violent one. The missionary era in which were born both the American and Chinese churches has ended. A new world civilization has emerged. Its form is blurred, but men and women in all parts of the world are living within it. Christians have been humbled and troubled by what they have seen and experienced. In both the United States and China, Christians are asking: To whom can we turn? What is the source of faith? What is our hope for the future? Why are we called to be missionaries to the ends of the earth to the end of time?

PART TWO

To Whom Shall We Turn?

CHAPTER 4

God Is
A Missionary God

"And he who sent me is with me; he has not left me alone ..."
(John 8:29).

*W*E live in an emerging world civilization. All men—white, black, yellow, brown, Hindu, Buddhist, Muslim, Communist, Christian—are being drawn together. Their personal lives—their culture, language, history—are converging into one common stream of human history. For the present, science and technology have become the freeway over which the heavy traffic of ideas moves. However, over the long run, as we have seen in an earlier chapter, other issues will have to be faced. Men and women in all parts of the world are seeking a deeper center to this new civilization than science or technics can provide. All men are asking or beginning to ask the question, "To whom or to what can we turn as a center for this new age?"

In such a world what are individual Christians to say and to do? How does this apply to the local congregation and to the work of the churches throughout the world? There are no simple answers. Furthermore, Christians do not agree among themselves as to just what is to be said and done. However, most Christians would, I think, agree that the following questions are the ones we must ask.

—Why are Christians missionary minded? What motivates them?
—What right does the Christian have to seek the conversion of the Jew, the secularist, the Communist, the Muslim, the Buddhist, and the Hindu?
—What is the uniqueness of the Church for this new age?
—What does it mean to witness to the presence of the Kingdom of God in the year 1963?

In this initial chapter we will be dealing with the question of motives. How do we explain the fact that the Christian church when alive and vibrant has always been missionary minded? What is the source of this motivation?

There is always the danger of supporting the missionary outreach of Christian faith for the wrong reasons. One danger is to be motivated by *pride*. This attitude is parodied in the sermon, "We are here on earth to help others; what on earth the others are here for I don't know." One reason why Protestant middle class churches find it difficult to serve the lower economic groups is the suspicion of those being served that they are pitied by the people above them socially and economically. Pity suggests someone reaching down to give a hand-out to those below. Where this is a motivation, even if unconscious, it is always resented. Too often when the collection plate is passed for a missionary cause, the motive for giving is of this nature. We must begin to think of the mission of the Church in terms of going to people who are *above* us. When we get that picture clearly in our minds, we will be able to guard ourselves against the motive of pity.

Another danger is being motivated by the *will to power*. An illustration is our frequent identification of the mission with anti-Communist programs. Communism is of course a serious menace. As a monolithic, totalitarian system it threatens not only the Christian but also *every* man, whatever his faith. But when the motive of anti-Communism is related to missionary thinking and evangelism, it is sterile. What it means is that our real interest is not in the people we are trying to evangelize. Actually we see them as a shield for our own protection. When those to whom we go sense this, they become suspicious of our motives and reject both the missionary and what he has to say.

A third danger is the motivation of *escape*. This is the temptation to think of a mission to a distant place in order to avoid facing difficult situations near at hand. For example, it is often a temptation for Christians struggling in their own neighborhood with a racial problem to turn their attention to Africa or Japan.

A Roman Catholic's Analysis of
Protestant Missionary Thought

We have learned from experience that motives of pride, the will to power, and escape are possible if we are not clear about the gospel.

The late Pierre Charles, a Roman Catholic professor, may not be the most objective critic of Protestant missionary thought, but even though his criticisms are often extreme and unfair, there is enough truth in what he says to warrant our careful attention. He believed that Protestant missionary thinking over the last 150 years is marked by four stages.[1]

The first came about the end of the 18th century during John Wesley's life. The motivation to a missionary concern, Professor Charles argues, was based on the *fear of God*. God was seen as a righteous Judge, harsh, heavy-handed with all who did not accept Jesus Christ. The other religions of the earth were seen as corrupt, and non-Christian lands were thought filled with foul pagans who needed cleansing.

By 1850 the thought had changed, writes Pierre Charles, to the *love of God*. God was seen as a kind Father, whose only desire was that all his children should be one. The God of judgment and damnation had retreated and given way to God the loving Father of all men.

By the time of the first world war, or somewhere in that period, the motivation had changed again, so Charles contends, to the *love of man*. God was now entirely out of the picture. The major purpose of missions was "a world community." There was a tremendous interest in feeding the poor, healing the sick, and teaching people to read.

Finally, writes Professor Charles, the motivation became the *fear of man*. Non-Christians were seen as potential Communists or potential revolutionists who needed conversion before they turned to the Communist world or before they started themselves to challenge the established social and economic order.

Whether Charles's analysis is fair or not, it is a reminder that in every generation Christians must get their bearings as to where they are and what the Scripture says to them about the gospel.

The 20th Century Theological Revolution

During the past forty years we have experienced in Protestantism what some have called a theological revolution. Men and women of all denominations have shared in this attempt to restate the

[1] J. W. Sweetman, "The Theological Basis of the Christian Mission" in *Papers on the Theology of Missions,* prepared for the Glen Lake (Michigan) Consultation Annual Report, Division of World Missions of the Board of Missions of The Methodist Church, 1957, pp. 36 ff. Professor Sweetman refers to Pierre Charles, *Les dossiers de l'action missionaire, Manuel de missionologie,* 2nd ed., Louvain, 1938.

gospel, which is "the same yesterday, today, and forever," into language that is understandable today.

Two men who played an important part in this development are Karl Barth and Hendrik Kraemer. Barth shook the theological world in 1918 with his *Commentary on Romans,* and in 1938 Hendrik Kraemer did the same for the missionary movement with his book, *The Christian Message in a Non-Christian World.* To understand what troubled both Barth and Kraemer is to remember the "theological erosion" referred to in the section on American Protestantism (p. 42). By the end of the 19th century there was a growing awareness of the emergence of a scientific world, and Christian theologians tried their best to adjust the gospel to a language of ideas that would make it meaningful. In the process of doing this, the Christian religion gradually became an expression of man's impulses toward God. Faith in God more and more became identified with what man felt he needed, rather than a response to God's activity toward man. The Scriptures increasingly became a book of instruction and inspiration to lead a good life. When Barth began to preach and later when Kraemer began to study the missionary movement, they became convinced that the gospel as understood in the New Testament was no longer the center of much of church life. What Nietzsche has prophesied in his parable of the "madman at noon" they found all too true. In the lives of many church people and even missionaries, the consciousness of God was fading. They still came to church but there was an emptiness in their lives. Barth and Kraemer turned, as did Luther and Wesley before them, to Scripture to discern again what it had to say about the relationship between God and man.

The Knowledge of God as Missionary

Why Should Anyone Want to Be a Missionary?

At some time or other the question has entered into all of our minds, "Why should anyone want to be a missionary?" "Why do we keep sending people to change other people's religion?" We may be thinking of a Buddhist in Hawaii, an animist in Bolivia, a Puerto Rican in New York City, a Muslim in Pakistan, a Hindu in India, or a Jewish family on our street. In an emerging world civilization, what is the source of our motivation to reach out to others?

They Are Not Invited

One thing is certain. Missionaries do not go because they are invited. George Webber writes of their experience in the East Harlem Protestant Parish in New York City:

It was very trying for the young clergy of East Harlem Protestant Parish in 1948 to discover how unwanted they really were by the community. Several times the clergy were mistaken for plain-clothes detectives or numbers men. Somebody sidled up to one of the staff and said out of the corner of his mouth, "Hey Bud, what is this? A new racket of Mark's to get hold of the people?" ("Mark," Vito Marcantonio, was then the left-wing congressman from East Harlem.) In a community which is predominately made up of minority groups a white face is almost automatically under suspicion. A white face may be a landlord, owner of one of the lousy tenements, a narcotics peddler, a gambler, or one of the professionals who come to "service the community." [2]

The experience is familiar to missionaries living in other parts of the world. From 1948 to 1958, when Communist terrorism in Malaya was at its height, there was only one road over the mountains to Pahang Province. It was a narrow, winding, forty-mile road that climbed up through the jungle to the top of the mountain range and then with tortuous curves dropped down to the jungle plain below. Each day Communist movements north and south had to cross this forty-mile strip. On this very road Sir Henry Guerney, the High Commissioner of Malaya, was ambushed and killed. Yet all through that ten-year period, ministers and missionaries alike crossed the mountains to Pahang. If there was to be a mission in the province of Pahang, there was no alternative. Who invited them to work in Pahang? It was obviously not the Communists living in the jungle. Nor was it the Muslims and the Chinese living on the other side. The Muslims of Malaya are a tightly knit community, and only a handful have become Christians. The Chinese are more responsive, but most of them are Buddhist or completely secularized and would shed no tears if the ministers, missionaries, and other Christians were to leave.

This, then, raises the question: Why do they go? Is it adventure? Is it blind obedience? Is it a kind of ecclesiastical imperialism? Is it pride? If so, it is hardly worth the price. A young Methodist

---

[2] George W. Webber, *God's Colony in Man's World* (New York: Abingdon Press, 1960), p. 83. Copyright 1960 by Abingdon Press.

missionary lost his life in Pahang Province in 1955. What is true in Malaya has been true in many parts of the world. The story is well known of the five young missionaries in Ecuador who in 1956 lost their lives to the primitive Auca Indians. A few years later, one of the wives with her little girl went up the river to live with the very tribe that had killed her husband. This is a strange twist. Why would she do it?

Four Partial Explanations

1. *The Great Commission*

A look at church history will provide some explanations. Some-missionaries have gone because they were convinced that the Great Commission[3] of Jesus, "All authority in heaven and on earth has been given to me. Go therefore and make disciples of all nations . . ." (Mt. 28:16-20) was meant for them. This was the explanation many would have given in the last century. Even today when a minister makes plans to preach a missionary sermon, it is this text that comes first to mind. The Great Commission is, of course, a valid motive. But to rely on one text as the source of all missionary conviction is precarious indeed. What if the papyrus scroll had been lost or the last chapter of Matthew muti-lated? Would this then rule out missionary obedience to the "ends of the earth" and to the end of time? The answer of course is No! From beginning to end, the New Testament is a missionary document. In some parts it puts the accent on a mission to the Jews alone; in other parts, mission to the whole inhabited world is the task. The Great Commission is a valid motive, but certainly we would not want to rest the entire case on one text.

2. *Human Compassion*

Others would interpret missionary obedience in terms of com-passion toward those in need. No one would argue that human compassion is not a legitimate motive. Yet human compassion as a motivation is hardly unique to the Christian experience. For the Buddhist, compassion for human life, in fact all of life, is an indispensable axiom of religion. Compassion alone has never been considered sufficient as a Christian motive. In fact it can sidetrack the Church into a program of humanitarianism that can vitiate if not destroy the cutting edge of missionary conviction.

---

[3] Stewart, *Thine Is the Kingdom*, pp. 11 ff. Dr. Stewart develops these four ideas of the Commission, Compassion, Community, and Continuity.

3. *A World Christian Community*

Still others would say that the vision of a world-wide Christian community motivates them. They would be understood. It is a valid motive. Certainly today there is a need for such a community of Christians throughout the world. It can be the cement to help hold the world together during these turbulent times. Here we see the persistent appeal of the Roman Catholic Church which makes this claim about itself as a world Christian community. Yet this motivation by itself is never an adequate explanation as to why we are to go to non-Christians. It takes our eyes off the solitary person to whom the gospel is directed, the dying African in the hospital bed, the Japanese college student seeking meaning for his life, the isolated mother in Alaska seeking comfort as she stands at her husband's grave.

4. *Continuity of the Church*

Finally, there are those who would express missionary obedience in terms of continuity. This is the motivation of loyalty to the past. There is the "endless line of splendor" of men and women who down through the years have given their lives to the Church. When the Church is described as an aircraft carrier plowing through the seas with planes flying from its decks, it is a legitimate description. The pilots learn that they are free to fly in any direction at any altitude, but they must always remember where the aircraft carrier is lest they be lost at sea when they run out of fuel. The Church's life is a valid motive to mission. The Roman Catholic Church gives a high priority to this kind of obedience. There is no doubt that church loyalty can put steel into the backbone of the missionary movement when confronting a dangerous period of history. Yet church history provides ample warning that denominational loyalty by itself is never a sufficient motive.

What Is a Deeper Motivation?

These answers of the Great Commission, human compassion, world Christian community, and the continuity of the Church are all partial explanations, but in themselves are insufficient. Where then can we look for the deeper meaning? What is the knowledge of God available to us in the Scripture that helps us understand the missionary task? Dr. D. T. Niles of Ceylon provides one clue. The gospel, he writes, has the characteristics of a whirlpool.

It pulls us first into its center and only then can it thrust us out into the mainstream of the world. Dr. Kenneth Scott Latourette, the historian, provides a more definite clue.

It is clear that at the very beginning of Christianity there must have occurred a vast release of energy, unequalled in the history of the race. Without it the future course of the faith is inexplicable. That burst of energy was ascribed by the early disciples to the founder of their faith. Something happened to the men who associated with Jesus. In his contact with them, in his crucifixion and in their assurance of his resurrection and of the continued living presence with his disciples of his spirit, is to be found the major cause of the success of Christianity.[4]

The Mission of the Triune God

These are important clues. But the motivation does not become real for us until we find ourselves responding to something beyond ourselves. We can speak of the One to whom we respond as *Christ*. His name has been on the lips of millions as they have gone through times of testing. We can speak of the One to whom we respond as the *Spirit* of God. Even when we cannot visualize him, his presence is felt. We can speak of the One to whom we respond as *God*. The word we use is not as critical as the recognition that missionary obedience is but an everyday response to what Christ, the Spirit, and God are doing in the world, in the Church, and in ourselves. P. T. Forsyth used to say, "There are three missionaries—the Father, the Son, and the Holy Spirit."

This is another way of saying that the mission in which we participate is the mission of the Triune God. It is not, in the first place, the mission of the Church or the mission of the Christian disciple. What we do or what the Church does is merely to respond to something that has been done by God Himself. When this becomes clear to us, we see that to refuse to enlist in the mission to all men is not just an issue of passing up the collection plate, but is a denial of Christian faith itself. Perhaps you know the story of the man in a morning worship service, who, upon receiving the collection plate, said to the usher, "I'm sorry. I do not believe in missions. I cannot give." Whereupon the usher whispered to him, "Then take some out. This collection is for you!"

---

[4] Kenneth Scott Latourette, *A History of the Expansion of Christianity. Volume I— The First Five Centuries* (New York: Harper & Row, Publishers, Inc., 1937), pp. 167-168. Copyright 1937 by Harper & Brothers.

The Love of Christ

Three Biblical pictures help us see how God works as a missionary. The first is a scene in a room in Jerusalem (Jn. 20:19-25). The doors are locked. The disciples are afraid. They fear for their lives; they are plagued by guilt because in the testing hour they fled. They are not sure what the next steps will be. Should they break up? Is the whole thing finished? Then something happens. Jesus comes into their midst. He looks at them and says, "Peace be with you" (Jn. 20:21).

The atmosphere of the room is immediately changed. Where there had been uncertainty, indecisiveness, and fear, there is electric hope and assurance. Jesus then shows them the wounds on his hands and feet. He stands before them as their humiliated leader, scorned and ridiculed by the world. Once they are assured of his presence with them, and reminded of his humiliation, he says to them, "As the Father has sent me, even so I send you." Then he breathes on them and says, "Receive the Holy Spirit."

The important point is that the motive to act—to go forth—was a response to what Christ had done for them. They were, in other words, incapable of thinking of a mission until they had been given assurance by Christ that his peace was theirs. This is the One who meets us when we enter into the world of Scripture. Christ is the missionary, but we cannot find the basic motive within ourselves until he comes to us, gives us assurance that he is alive, and reminds us of his humiliation and death. Then the words become meaningful, "As the Father has sent me, even so I send you" (Jn. 20:21).

The Freedom of the Spirit

The second scene concerns the Holy Spirit. Peter has just come down from the rooftop at Joppa where he has had a remarkable dream. A voice said to him, "Rise, Peter; kill and eat" (Acts 10:13). When Peter declined, as a good Jew would, the voice answered, "What God has cleansed you must not call unclean." Immediately there is a knock at the door. The servants of Cornelius, the Gentile, arrive asking for an audience with Peter. The next day Peter goes with them to the home of Cornelius. There he hears that the Holy Spirit descended upon the family. "Truly I perceive," he says, "that God shows no partiality" (Acts 10:34). Peter then preached to them the same sermon he preached at Pentecost.

As he spoke, the Holy Spirit descended upon the entire household. Peter faced a difficult decision. Should he or should he not baptize them? They were not Jews. His response was immediate. "Can any one forbid water for baptizing these people who have received the Holy Spirit as we have?" (Acts 10:47.) A few days later he reported the whole matter to the other Apostles, explaining why he had baptized the Gentile family. They accepted his explanation as to what the Holy Spirit had done: "Then to the Gentiles also God has granted repentance unto life!" they said (Acts 11:18).

We are learning afresh in our time that the power of the mission of Christian faith is found in the life of the Holy Spirit. Yet the characteristic of the Spirit is that he leads us to affirm faith in Christ and in God but never in himself. The Spirit is always self-effacing. This is one reason why it has been so difficult to develop a systematic theology concerning the Spirit. Here again there are three points to remember. First, the early church understood the motive of its mission always as a response to what the Spirit was doing. Second, humility is the mark of the Holy Spirit's life. Third, the Holy Spirit is free. When you think he will come from the right side to speak, he comes from the left. And when we turn to the left, expecting him there, he comes from the right. The Holy Spirit is like the wind. Try to put it in a bag and its life is gone. It is like a sunbeam through a window— pull the shade to keep it in the room and it disappears. The Church has learned again and again that when it lives by the Spirit, always it finds freedom to change.

The Sovereignty of God

The third picture speaks of God. It is not really a picture, for no man can see God. It is more in the form of a report of a conversation. Moses wanted to know God. Straightaway came the reply, "I AM WHO I AM" (Ex. 3:14), or as it has been translated by another, "I will manifest to be that which I will manifest myself to be." The startling word is "I." God is the hidden God, but he is not a principle or some kind of energy. He is the "I AM." "I am the God of your father, the God of Abraham, the God of Isaac. . . . I have seen the affliction of my people . . . and have heard their cry . . . and I have come down to deliver them" (Ex. 3:6 ff.). He is not the creature of man, but the Lord of

66

history. His ways are not our ways. He is the Sovereign God, the One God. If it is true that there is but one God, and if he is the God revealed in Jesus Christ and through the work of the Holy Spirit, then a world mission follows from this. The sovereignty of God remains, then, the central affirmation of any missionary theology. One cannot live in the world of the Scripture and not sense his power. He can use Assyria as a rod to punish Israel and then break the rod in two. The Scripture is a constant reminder that we cannot trade with God as Adam and Eve tried to do. He is God, the "I AM," who holds us accountable for what we do as individuals and what we do in the life of the Church. Yet we never discover the full knowledge of God that moves the human heart until we see him as the suffering God of love who expects humility because he has humbled himself.

The Cross as the Place Where Love, Freedom, and Power Meet

One of the most moving passages in contemporary literature is found in Arnold Toynbee's sixth volume of his *Study of History*. He points out that in times of disintegration and change, creative individuals are called to play the role of a savior. He deals with a number of types. There is the savior with the sword, the savior who is a philosopher, and the many varieties who are gods. After studying many he concludes:

And this is in truth the final result of our survey of saviours. When we first set out on this quest we found ourselves moving in the midst of a mighty marching host; but as we have pressed forward on our way the marchers, company by company, have been falling out of the race. The first to fail were the swordsmen, the next the archaists, the next the futurists, the next the philosophers, until at length there were no more human competitors left in the running. . . . At the final ordeal of death, few even of these would-be saviour gods, have dared to put their title to the test by plunging into the icy river. And now, as we stand and gaze with our eyes fixed upon the farther shore, a single figure rises from the flood and straightway fills the whole horizon. There is the Saviour; "and the pleasure of the Lord shall prosper in his hand. He shall see the travail of his soul, and shall be satisfied." [5]

When we study the Scriptures we are reminded that no man has ever seen God. He can be addressed, but he is never seen. He

[5] Arnold J. Toynbee, *A Study of History* (London: Oxford University Press, 1939), Volume VI, p. 278.

is the sovereign Lord, the one who scatters his stars across the heavens with the ease that we throw a handful of sand into the air. Yet when the knowledge of God as missionary becomes clear to us, it includes more than his sovereignty. We also think of the life, death, and resurrection of Jesus and the continuing presence of the Holy Spirit. All these manifestations of the living God, when they draw close to us, withdraw their power, coming to us in humility and weakness. It is in response to this knowledge of God that missionary obedience is born.

In the first part of this book we were reminded that there are mysteries about God's redemptive purpose for mankind. There are many riddles we have not been able to resolve. We have no final word as to when or even how the purpose will be accomplished. We cannot be certain that the Church will ever be more than a small percentage of the world's population. We must live by faith that God's purpose is revealed in Jesus Christ and is now being fulfilled through the Spirit, using men and women of every race and nation living within the fellowship of the Church, who are willing to respond in obedience. But the Church is not the missionary, nor are the people within it. The missionary is God at work in the world, seeking reconciliation between man and himself and inviting us to participate in what is first of all *his* task.

It is my firm conviction that nothing less than this realization will provide the depth of understanding essential for the half century ahead. Dietrich Bonhoeffer, the German pastor hanged by the Nazis, sensed the depth of our need when he said, "We do not know what to do, but our eyes are upon Him!"

CHAPTER 5

Faith
Means Witness

"You shall be my witnesses . . ." (Acts 1:8).

*I*N this emerging world civilization, when people throughout the earth are seeking a common center to provide meaning for this "one world," the testimony of the Christian is that this center is Jesus Christ. To support this testimony Christians submit three observations about mankind.

All Men Desire "To Be," "To Belong," "To Do"

Every man desires "to be" someone, to be recognized as a person who has value.

Every man feels a need "to belong" with those who will accept him as an equal.

Every man desires "to do" something that will give purpose to his life.

These three words "to be" (*our selfhood*), "to belong" (*our need for fellowship*), and "to do" (*our desire to be relevant*) provide a bond among all men.

When we talk about Jesus Christ as the source of man's hope we must relate his life, death, and resurrection to these common human hungers of "being," "belonging," and "doing." When all these have been met, we can speak of the whole man being redeemed.

All Men Experience Anxiety

Not only have men and women discovered common desires, but also they realize that they are experiencing the same kind of anxiety. It is dangerous to generalize; but if there is any one word that describes mankind's spiritual plight today, it is "meaninglessness." Paul Tillich writes that no one word makes clearer the sickness of modern man.

One reason for this is the fantastic and terrifying complexity of the modern world. We recall the picture of men and women being swept along by the swift river of technological change. The river is carrying them toward an unknown destination. Is the end to be nuclear destruction or a new day of promise? The speed and totality of change have left millions of people bewildered and confused.

A second explanation comes not from the world outside but from the deep recesses of the mind and heart. Those who have lived close to Hindus, Buddhists, and Muslims are aware that they are experiencing the same feeling of meaninglessness and emptiness. Furthermore, distinctions of race, class, or age do not alter fundamentally man's deep needs. In the past we have used the words "death," "guilt," and "sin" to describe man's illness. They still hold true. But we can add three other words: "anxiety," "dread," and "frustration."

Anxiety: It is like a deep pit where light cannot penetrate. Anxiety is felt by every man. The experience is like a nightmare. We awaken, frightened and restless. Once awake, we cannot remember what frightened us. Yet we are aware that something is wrong within us. This restlessness may be partly childhood conditioning, but it may be also a warning that at the center of our lives is not God, but ourselves.

Dread: Higher in the consciousness than anxiety is dread. There is dread of death. This is the experience of every man. When in danger or near death men yearn to go on living, to see their home again, to be with their loved ones and friends. The testimony of all men is that life is good and should not be surrendered. Yet men know that they must give it up. When a baby is born, the child is already old enough to die, and eventually will. There is no way to escape what lies ahead. So all men dread what they know is inevitable.

If our only dread was of death, much of man's burden could be lifted. But there is more than this. Men are afraid not only of death; the majority are afraid of life. Where the fear of life dominates the mind of a person, he or she is a candidate for a mental breakdown or suicide. This condition fortunately is that of the few. Yet the lives of many are weighed down by fear of failure or the burden of themselves.

When we speak of dread of death and life, we are trying to locate the spiritual problem of mankind. We find at the very center of the goodness of life two persistent challenges to every man's existence—death and life. These two challenges plague and harass man's every step, whether he be a Hindu, Buddhist, Communist, or Christian.

Frustration: Unlike anxiety and dread, which are in the subconscious, frustration is at the surface, expressing itself in irritation, feelings of guilt, restlessness, anger, prejudice, hate, and fear. Friends tell us that there is really nothing to worry about. Yet our plans never work out as we would like. No matter where we reach, we do not seem to arrive. What we see in our personal lives we see in national life. There is always an incompleteness about the world. No matter how generous we are with other nations, no matter how hard we work to help them, they do not seem to understand us or trust us. So our frustration grows.

These manifestations of spiritual illness—anxiety, dread, frustration—are in all men. An African leaves his tribal home and goes to the city to work, thinking this will end his frustration. He finds his problems are not resolved but intensified.

The same is true of Americans living in suburbia, Japanese in Hokkaido, and Brazilians in Brasilia. For many this feeling of lostness, meaninglessness, and emptiness is a "hell" on earth. Powerful forces seem to thwart their every move.

Kafka's book, *The Trial,* is a parable not only for the Western world but also for all mankind. In Kafka's story a man is arrested. He is taken to prison. No charges are leveled against him, yet he is to be shot the next morning. The execution takes place. Why did he die? It doesn't make sense. That is the point of the book. In the world in which we live there is much that doesn't make sense. There is enough food for all, but many are hungry. With resources sufficient to create a new world of security we stand on the brink of disaster. In this situation men and women the world over seek salvation from the gnawing, growing sense of the meaninglessness of their lives and the future of mankind.

A New Spirit Is Evident

Because Christians share the common predicament of mankind, they may have a new spirit as they look at other religions. The right of Christians to go out as missionaries is challenged not only by Hindus and Muslims, but also by Christians. What are we to say? There is no easy answer. One statement, however, can be made immediately: Christians have no more right to go to a Hindu or a Muslim than the Hindu or the Muslim has to seek to convert Christians. That is the point. In this new era of world history every man has not only the right but also the responsibility of sharing with others what he believes to be the meaning of human existence. The issues are important. All men are asking the question, To whom or to what can we turn as the center of our common existence? In this setting every man —the Buddhist, the Hindu, the Christian—must share what he holds that center to be. Christians have as much right as anyone else to witness to their faith, but they should remember with shame the arrogance so often manifest in their past relationship with other religions. Nothing is uglier than spiritual pride and the will to power cloaked in self-righteousness. To deduce that all who do not agree with Christians are damned is, in my judgment, a perversion of Christian love.

Nicolas Berdyaev has stated this vividly: "People managed to deduce from Christianity the most disgusting morality that has ever been known—the morality of transcendental heavenly egoism. 'The good' are so anxious to get into the Kingdom of Heaven that in the crush at the entrance to it they are ready to trample on a great number of their neighbors and push them down to hell, to eternal damnation. . . . This is the worst defeat that Christianity has suffered in human hearts." [1]

Witness Before Argument

Fortunately, a change has come in the minds of Christians about their mission and their relationship to other Christians and non-Christians. One can see this in the Roman Catholic Church. Roman Catholics increasingly are admitting that those outside the visible Roman Catholic Church are not automatically outside the sphere of salvation. This has made possible a new conversation between Protestants and Roman Catholics.

There is also a growing awareness among Protestants that they need more openness of spirit when asking what will happen to Hindus, Buddhists, and Muslims. For example, Dr. Reinhold Niebuhr writes of the "hidden Christ" who operates within the world, making possible conversion of a man to Christ in ways that as yet we cannot understand.[2] There are many signs of this

[1] Nicolas Berdyaev, *The Destiny of Man* (New York: Harper & Row, Publishers, Inc., 1937), pp. 146-147.
[2] John C. Bennett, "Christ and Non-Christians," *Christianity and Crisis* (May 15, 1961), p. 74.

new spirit within the Protestant churches. The problem is how to maintain this openness of mind and at the same time avoid the creeping death that comes to the Christian faith when we start talking about all religions being the same. Religions are *not* the same. Any fair reading of the Old and New Testaments is a reminder that the Christian has no alternative but to make a particular claim for Jesus Christ. Where Christians lose this realization of the uniqueness of Christ for *all* men, they lose with it the urgency to preach the gospel to all men. More than that, they are rejecting the central affirmation of the Christian faith.

There is no easy answer to this problem. One point seems clear. In the emerging world civilization Christians have both the right and the responsibility to witness to Jesus Christ. The important point is not to argue dogma or creed with the Jew, the Muslim, the Communist, the Hindu and Buddhist, but rather to witness to what the Christian knows from his experience to be true. If the Christian can make clear through his words and his life that through faith in Christ he has "become" a new person, he will have something to say. On the other hand, if in his own life he has not found himself "to be" someone new, his words will make little contribution to the contemporary conversation among the great religions.

The Witness of Faith

The Christian recognizes that there are many questions we cannot answer. We do not know for sure when God's mission began; nor do we know how or when it is going to end. We cannot prove in language acceptable in a law court that the Christian faith is better than others. This does not mean that we should not make comparisons, for religions are different. But these comparisons will never be decisive. All this is a reminder that we must continue to live by faith

—that God has a plan that all men shall find wholeness, fullness, and meaning for their lives;
—that this plan is revealed in the life, teaching, crucifixion and resurrection of Jesus;
—that the plan is being fulfilled by the Spirit of God using the lives of people (which we call the Church), who are witnesses to the impact of Jesus Christ on their lives.

73

It is this theme that Paul develops in his letters. This is, in fact, the theme of all New Testament preaching. It is evident in the sermons of Peter at Pentecost (Acts 2:14-42) and in the home of Cornelius (Acts 10:34-43). It is the theme of Stephen's defense before a hostile crowd (Acts 7). It is the theme of Paul's preaching in Athens (Acts 17:22-31). It is not surprising to find the same theme in the letters of Paul. His life is instructive for us.

Paul, the Missionary

Paul is the most famous missionary in the New Testament. His travels up and down the Mediterranean were like those of Francis Asbury crisscrossing the eastern and southern part of the United States. In Paul's life we see three convictions.

There was first his sense of *obedience*. "I feel," he said, "as if I were under an obligation." Second, he was convinced that *suffering* was an inevitable part of obedience. He was therefore able to identify his suffering with that of Christ. His words to the Galatians, "I bear on my body the marks of Jesus," were not idle words. Finally, there was his conviction that *the final outcome of all his efforts was in God's hands.* Thus he could stop briefly in Athens or Corinth and leave without fear of failure. However, if we see only these three factors in Paul's life, we miss his secret. Beneath his obedience, suffering, and willingness to leave the outcome to God we see something else. It is to that we must turn. Fifty years ago scholars were suggesting that Paul did not represent the thinking of the other disciples in his understanding of Christian faith. Today there is almost unanimous agreement among scholars that what Paul considered of primary importance was held so by others in the Church.

Paul was not only one of the great missionaries of the Church, he was also one of its great minds. His perception into the center of man's spiritual predicament remains today a marvel of understanding. He saw all men living in one of two conditions: they lived in a world either *prior* to faith or *under* faith. The question is whether or not this distinction is relevant for our day.

Man's Condition Prior to Faith

"So with us," Paul wrote to the Galatians, "when we were children, we were slaves to the elemental spirits of the universe" (Gal. 4:3). Immediately we ask what this has to do with the world in which we live. How does it help explain the incompleteness of life experienced by all men? How does it help men and women of every culture and race to understand why they cannot live the lives they want to live? How does Paul's analysis of man help us see more clearly the nature of mankind's frustration today?

The key word in Paul's diagnosis of man's sickness is the word "flesh." For Paul, to live in the "flesh" is to live without God. This means that at the center of one's life is not God but oneself. This orientation of mental, physical, and emotional energy around ourselves leads to all kinds of perversions. Paul's language includes the words "death," "sin," and "guilt." They are still meaningful. The words "anxiety," "dread," "frustration," and "meaninglessness" say the same thing. (See p. 70 above.)

This is no academic statement. We have learned from bitter experience that Christians can fall back into a world prior to faith. When they do, perversions are sure to follow.

Those who have read the novel *Exodus* will remember the description of the reception center in a Nazi extermination camp. Truck after truck loaded with Jewish men and women arrived at the center. After unloading, the people were ushered into the room. There they were divided into groups. The children, the old, the weak, the pregnant were immediately segregated for the gas chambers. The adults were ordered to put their arms above their heads so that the children could be stuffed in around their legs. The doors were then closed, the gas turned on. By the millions they died.

The appalling point is that it was university-trained minds that conceived and worked out the techniques of extermination. More than that, most of the planners and those who actually did the killing were baptized Christians. In horror we ask: How could well-educated, cultured, baptized Christians participate in barbarism of this kind? How could their values have been so distorted? What happened in Germany is a reminder of what is possible in every land where all men living unto themselves begin to worship "elemental spirits."

Man's Life under Faith

If this is mankind's situation prior to faith, what is it under faith? In Paul's conversion experience are three important lessons for every person concerned with the Christian mission today:

1. *Faith Is Trust and Self-Surrender*

Recalling his experience on the road to Damascus, Paul wrote, "A man is not justified by works of the law but through faith in Jesus Christ" (Gal. 2:16). There are Biblical scholars who suggest that whenever Paul thought of his conversion experience, as he did frequently, the imagery of the Genesis story of creation came into his mind. He felt as if his life had been without form and void (emptiness) and the darkness was upon the face of the deep (meaninglessness); then the Spirit of God moved over the face of the waters, and God said, "Let there be light," and there was light. The light as Paul understood it was the sudden realization that what God required of him was not that his theology should be correct, or his life perfect, or his reputation unsmirched, but that all he had to do was throw himself with reckless abandon into God's care and trust him. For Paul this was a radically new idea, but he discovered in it an alternative to meaninglessness and despair. It provided for him a freedom, both of action and thought, that he was to maintain to his death.

The renewal of the churches throughout the world has been made possible by this rediscovery in our time of the meaning of faith. If we think of the Christian faith as a bag to be filled with a set of correct doctrines and creeds, it is impossible to understand what Paul is saying to our day. Faith is not the "faith of our fathers" or "I accept the statement of the Church"; it is a relationship, a giving of one's self to God in trust and confidence. This has never been easy for Christians to accept. Many would rather live by rules and laws as do the Muslims. But the Christian faith is like a parachute jump or a high dive. It is an act of courage. Never has there been a time when it demanded any more courage than it does today. But our experience is that when the leap *is* made it opens up a new world of meaning. We see God in new light. We see ourselves also in a new perspective and find ourselves in a different relationship to our neighbor.

2. *Faith Comes from a Personal Encounter with God*

In this emerging world civilization, to say that God speaks directly to a person is to give an importance to each man that has radical implications. This Paul recognized as the center of his own conversion experience. There were those who challenged Paul's right to be an apostle. His answer was, "I did not receive it from man, . . . but it came through a revelation of Jesus Christ" (Gal. 1:12). This declaration of Paul's that he was a freeman in Christ, an apostle like the others, is important to recover in the life of the Church.

Those within the early Church who opposed Paul feared this freedom he was claiming for himself. Their disagreement was theological but their attack was personal. First, they said, he was a neurotic, a poor team man, a most inadequate speaker, and subject to illness. Their second charge was more damaging. They argued that he had no right to speak with any authority for the simple reason that he was not an apostle.

Even at that early time it was held by some that the ultimate authority was with the apostles. They were the ones who handed the faith to the other disciples. The requirement of being an apostle was to have been with Jesus, to have been commissioned by him an apostle, and to have witnessed the Resurrection. Paul, of course, did not fulfill these requirements. Paul immediately saw the critical issue. It is the same issue that we are facing in *our* generation. Paul saw these devout and committed Christian men and women leading the Church back into the legalistic world of Judaism. He went to great pains to point out from the autobiography of his life that his authority came from his conversion and not from the other apostles. By this he did not mean that he could think anything he wanted to about Christ. Again and again he checked with the other disciples to make certain he was not on a tangent. In I Cor. 15:3 he made it clear that he saw his role as one who "delivered what he had received."

Important as this was, it was secondary to the more critical issues of the authority of the Christian experience of faith in God. Paul pointed out that he simply could not have received either his understanding of faith or his commission to be a missionary from the other apostles. First of all, he never met the apostles until three years after his conversion (Gal. 1:17, 18), and then only Peter and James. Second, it was not until fourteen years later that he saw them again. If they still had any doubts as to his independence, he recalled the argument he had with Peter in Antioch. There he had called Peter down publicly for not eating with the Gentiles (Gal. 2:11-16).

77

In his letter to the Galatians, Paul stresses again and again the point that his missionary life came out of his personal relationship with Jesus Christ. He had seen the Risen Christ as clearly as any other apostle. He had received from Christ his commission. It takes courage for us to affirm as did Paul that the source of our authority comes not from the Church, or from our parents, but from our personal act of trust when we stand before God. In this affirmation, but especially in the act of trust, we discover that we are important to God.

3. *Faith Is an Experience of Sonship*

Paul wrote to the Galatians:

But when the time had fully come, God sent forth his Son, born of woman, born under the law, to redeem those who were under the law, so that we might receive adoption as sons. And because you are sons, God has sent the Spirit of his Son into our hearts crying "Abba, Father." So through God you are no longer a slave but a son, and if a son then an heir. (Gal. 4:4-7.)

After his conversion Paul realized that the crucial question facing the early Church was not the incidents of Jesus' life remembered by the disciples, but the meaning of his total life. When Paul wrote, "God sent his son to redeem us," he was dealing with more than the incidents of a man's life. In his conversion, like a flash of light it dawned upon him that this was the one for whom the people of Israel had waited. In the life, crucifixion, and resurrection of Jesus, Paul saw God identifying himself with mankind for a purpose. The purpose was that men would discover God as a Father and in that discovery would see themselves as his sons, and their fellow men as their brothers. For Christians this is the fulfillment of meaning of the words "to be."

This has taken place not only in the past. Nor is it seen only in intellectual discussion.

An up-to-date story from the streets of New York dramatically points up how the dynamics of Christian faith can be understood. In his moving account of his work among juvenile gangs in New York, Episcopalian C. Kilmer Myers writes of Willie, a Negro boy:

We had just finished dinner in the Vicarage one Sunday afternoon, and the clergy had gone. Only a few parishioners remained to talk awhile. Suddenly we heard shouting in the street, the voices were angry. Rushing to the window, we looked out upon a large group of the Knights standing in front of the Settlement. When they saw us they pointed down the street.

Up the middle of Henry Street, up by the bloody block, as some have named it, came the two Johnson brothers. They walked slowly, their hands in their pockets. They looked grim.

I gestured inquiringly with my hands and shoulders at the Knights. One of them shouted, "Razors!"

I tore down into the street and walked toward the approaching brothers feeling half foolish, as though I were a part of a Western drama played in the main street of a cattle town. But it was serious, and I was not sure how to cope with it. I knew only that I must somehow get the razors away from them.

I used every argument I could think of to get the razors. I warned them of the punishment that certainly would follow a cutting. I reminded them that they both had records and that this time they would be sent away for a long time. Were they to kill one of the Knights, they too might pay with their lives. I knew I was not reaching either of them, although at times Willie seemed to waver. I sensed that he really wanted me to help him out of the fix they were in.

Finally, I said to him, "Willie, what do you call me?"

After a moment of hesitation, he answered, "Father."

"Willie, what do the other Knights call me?"

A longer silence and then, "Father."

This time I waited; it was my last pitch.

"Willie, if you call me Father, what does that mean that you are to me?"

He looked as though he wanted to cry, "I, I am . . . your son."

"And they?"

"Sons."

We looked at each other, long. His was a soft look, that of a child. Slowly he reached into his pocket. He pulled out the razor and handed it to me. Then he turned and, with Ben, walked away down the street.[3]

In a city street where the anxiety of meaninglessness is so pronounced, the simple dynamics of faith is still possible. Willie could see it only dimly. But he could communicate with Father Myers because he trusted him. Having trusted him, he could then understand the meaning of fatherhood. Having recognized

[3] C. Kilmer Myers, *Light the Dark Streets* (Greenwich, Connecticut: The Seabury Press, 1957), pp. 32 ff. Copyright 1957 by The Seabury Press.

fatherhood, he could sense what sonship meant; and out of that came recognition of his relationship to others. There is another point to the story that we should not miss. Father Myers would never have been living in that neighborhood save for missionary obedience and the courage to affirm his faith in Jesus Christ.

The Courage to Affirm the
Finality of Christ for All Men

In an emerging technological world civilization it takes the courage of faith to believe and confess the uniqueness of Christ. It is the confidence and trust that God has acted and spoken once for all in Jesus Christ.

This was the testimony of the disciples. For John, Mark, Luke, Paul, Timothy, and the others Christ was the midpoint in the hourglass. Sand moving from the top to the bottom has to pass this midpoint; and if you turn the glass over, the same is true of the sand as it flows from whence it came. It is also the testimony of Christians today. It takes courage to believe that of all the lives that have ever been lived on this earth, like particles of sand stretching for miles along the shore, mankind is to examine *one* life to see the possibilities of all the others. It takes courage to say that of all the years that have swept through history, men and women of every culture need to look at three years to understand them all. It takes courage to think that of all the suffering that has touched human hearts—pain, failure, torture, death— Hindus, Buddhists, and Muslims must with us examine one twenty-four hour period to probe the mystery of all the rest. It takes courage to tell the Communists that of all the joy that has brought hope to men and women, the height of joy is never understood until they see two women standing at an empty tomb. We obviously cannot share this with others unless we have experienced it ourselves. Nor can we share it unless it comes to us fresh every morning.

Each morning we need to hear again the words, "Born of a woman, born under the law, and God sent his Son to redeem us." As we hear these words, the Holy Spirit helps us again to form on our lips, "Abba, Father." It is in the discovery of the Fatherhood of God made possible in the light of the face of Jesus Christ, renewed every day, that we see our own sonship and what we can become.

We say with the writer of John's Gospel, "But these are written that you may believe that Jesus is the Christ, the Son of God, and that believing you may have life in His name" (Jn. 20:31).

To Sum Up

Every man and woman has a right to hear what a fellow human being believes to be the way of salvation from emptiness and meaninglessness. In the emerging new age every man has not only the right but also the responsibility to speak. Every man and woman has the capacity to understand the message of God's coming to the world in Jesus Christ. This does not mean they will accept it, but that all have the capacity to understand. Every man and woman has an invitation to make a decision of "yes" or "no." The Christian cannot force such an answer from another, but he is responsible that his own answer is "yes."

CHAPTER 6

The Church
As a Summons to a
New Humanity

"Of his own will he brought us forth by the word of truth that we should be a kind of first fruits of his creatures" (James 1:18).

*I*N this emerging world civilization men are discovering that their common humanity includes not only a desire "to be" someone but a desire "to belong." All men share in common a need to belong to families, social clubs, political parties, labor unions, and religious associations.

But when we say people want "to belong" what is it they want to belong to? Many answers could be given. For our purposes only three things need be mentioned.

First, men want to belong to a group that knows why it exists. This is obvious. To belong to a group that has no purpose whatsoever is a waste of time.

Second, men want to belong to a group that is inclusive. After they themselves are inside the group, they may then encourage exclusiveness. But before they are in, they want it to be inclusive.

Third, men want to belong to a group that challenges them to a higher way of life.

If these three observations are valid, many Christian churches would immediately find themselves under indictment.

If it is true that men want to belong to a group that knows why it exists, where does this leave many Christian churches? Why does the Church exist? Is its purpose to provide fellowship, ethical guidance, and comfort on Sunday morning? Or does it exist as a missionary summons to all who do not believe in Jesus Christ?

If it is true that men want to belong to a group that is inclusive, what does this say to the average local congregation? Is the Church a club, a gathering of like-minded people? Or is it a group that crosses cultural, class, and racial lines? If it is not inclusive, what right does it have to make a claim that it can provide the center of the emerging world civilization?

Finally, if it is true that men want to belong to a group that calls them to a distinctive way of life, what is the implication for American Christians? One observer has pointed out that the weakness in so much of contemporary American Protestantism is that the lives of the people who go to church are not noticeably different from the lives of those who are never there. What distinctive style of life is required of a Christian in this emerging civilization?

If it is true that all men desire "to belong" to groups that know why they exist, are inclusive, and call their members to a distinctive style of life, we can see three norms by which men can measure the relevance of the Church for the time in which we live.

The Church Exists as a Summons to Faith

The critical missionary issue facing the Church is to discover anew why it exists. Of all the early Christian leaders only Paul saw the radical uniqueness of the Christian Church. Only he was sufficiently aware of the old to recognize the new. Paul was a scholar of the Old Testament. In his letters he quotes from 141 different chapters in the Old Testament. He was therefore able to understand as did no other early Church leader the emergence of the New Testament Church in terms of the Old Testament. The Old Testament for Paul, as for Luther, was the cradle in which the New Testament was born.

For Paul the crucial person of the Old Testament was Abraham. A leading missionary scholar, Dr. M. A. C. Warren, General Secretary of the Church Missionary Society in London, writes that Abraham was in reality the first missionary. What he means is that our mission as Christians began with Abraham's call from God to go forth into an unknown world. The call included all people of the earth. It was a world missionary call.

Now Jehovah said unto Abram, Get thee out of thy country, and from thy kindred and from thy father's house, unto the land that I will show thee: and I will make of thee a great nation, and I will bless thee, and make thy name great; . . . and in thee shall all the families of the earth be blessed (Genesis 12:1-3, American Standard Version).

In another passage we find these words:

84

After these things the word of the Lord came to Abram in a vision, "Fear not, Abram, I am your shield; your reward shall be very great." But Abram said, "O Lord God, what wilt thou give me, for I continue childless. . . ." And he brought him outside and said, "Look toward heaven, and number the stars, if you are able to number them." Then he said to him, "So shall your descendants be." And he believed the Lord . . . (Genesis 15:1-6, Revised Standard Version).

This conversation is followed by the story of Isaac's birth and the instruction to Abraham, "Take your son and kill him." Søren Kierkegaard wrote that if Abraham had been a man of religion he would have left his son at home and gone to the mountain and offered himself as a substitute by thrusting the knife into his own chest. But, said Kierkegaard, Abraham was a man of faith. He trusted God and prepared to do as he was told.

We must look behind the story of the offering of Isaac to see that it had a meaning for Paul and also for us today. The story reveals a test of Abraham's qualification to be a missionary to all the peoples of the earth. Was he or was he not a man who could trust God in all things? For Paul this was the great moment in Israel's history, surpassed only by the Incarnation of Christ. For Paul the mission of Abraham was to go to all the earth. This was the reason why the people of Israel had been set apart. They existed for a purpose. The purpose was a missionary one. As a Jewish scholar, however, Paul realized that Abraham's missionary concern had been forgotten by the people of Israel.

In the Old Testament beyond the Abraham story there are three books that focus attention on all the nations as a legitimate concern of Israel. In the latter part of Isaiah (Chapters 40–55) there is the vision of Israel serving as a suffering servant for the nations. This theme is restated in Jonah's reluctant preaching trip to Nineveh. Lastly, we see the same theme developed in the Book of Daniel. In other words, the mission given to and accepted by Abraham had been over the centuries misunderstood. Paul put the blame on Jewish law and temple ritual. This reliance, he argued, had turned Israel in upon itself. Instead of becoming a world-wide mission it had become a national religion. God had become the God of the nation. Israel had in its concern for itself become incapable of understanding the purpose for which it had been created.

For Paul the coming of Jesus meant that this central reason for Israel's existence had been restored. "As the Father hath sent me, so send I you," said Jesus to the disciples in the upper room. In like manner when Peter reported the outcome of his trip to the home of Cornelius, the Gentile, the disciples said, "Then to the Gentiles also God has granted repentance unto life" (Acts 11:18).

One only has to read the Book of Acts to see what early Christians considered the purpose of their communal life. It was a summons to faith—

> God has fulfilled his promise.
> The Messiah has come.
> Repent and believe the good news.

In 1791 a Methodist preacher wrote in his diary, "As long as I have strength, let me travel; as long as I have breath, let me praise thee." [1] As Emil Brunner has put it, "The Church exists for mission as the fire exists for burning." If we expect our children or those in other cultures "to belong" to the Church, they must have a personal understanding of why it exists. Paul reminds us that it exists as a people set apart as a summons to call men to faith in God who has revealed himself in Jesus Christ. That is why it was created.

The Church as a Summons to an Inclusive Community

Not only must a group know why it exists, but it must also be inclusive. At the end of the third chapter of Galatians there is a remarkable passage. In all of classical literature there is nothing to compare with it. The passage reads, "For as many of you as were baptized into Christ have put on Christ. There is neither Jew nor Greek, there is neither slave nor free, there is neither male nor female; for you are all one in Christ Jesus" (3:27, 28).

In his mind's eye Paul saw emerging in the world a unique fellowship. It was unique not merely because it was inclusive. Other religions are that. Its inclusiveness was possible through common love and loyalty to a person named Jesus Christ. As Paul looked around the Mediterranean world, he saw this emerging community including both Jews and Gentiles, free men and slaves, and men and women. Other communities remained the same; but this was new.

Paul had an astonishing explanation as to the cause of this. To the Gentiles he said: ". . . remember that you were . . . alienated

---
[1] Quoted by Bishop Hazen G. Werner in a speech given in Chicago, July 1962.

from the commonwealth of Israel . . . But now in Christ Jesus you who once were far off have been brought near in the blood of Christ. For he is our peace, who has made us both one, and has broken down the dividing wall of hostility . . ." (Eph. 2:12-14). To the Jews he said the same thing. What Paul saw in Christ was the love of God shattering the walls that divided the Jew and Gentile (*the political problem* of that day), the free man and the slave (*the social problem*), and men and women (*the cultural problem*).

Paul could understand what had happened because he had experienced the change of attitudes in his own life. Whereas Gentiles had been "outsiders," as a Christian he found he could be closer to a Gentile than to fellow-Jews. Something had happened to revolutionize his point of view. This revolution has continued down through the centuries.

Christians again and again, as the people of Israel before them, have rebelled against this inclusiveness. We continue to rebel today. But in our better moments we know that the Church *does* include all men. When Christ is at the center of a Christian's life he can accept people of every race and age. Dr. C. F. Andrews, one of the great missionaries to India, was a long-time friend of Mahatma Gandhi. One day a student asked Dr. Andrews about his relationship to Gandhi in comparison to his relationship with a Christian. Dr. Andrews thought for a moment. Then he said, "When I kneel at the communion table of my Lord Jesus Christ and beside me is an illiterate Indian peasant I have never seen before, I am closer to him than I could be or ever have been to Gandhi, my friend." This is not a sentimental thought. It is a hard saying and cuts deep. It is a judgment on any Christian who feels closer to those in his own class or race who are not Christian than he does to a person of another race or class who is a Christian. It seems clear that God will not browbeat us into change, but we are learning that unless we change, the world will not see the uniqueness of the Church as a summons to an inclusive community in Seoul, Manila, Cairo, Johannesburg, London, and Chicago.

The Church as a Summons to a Distinctive and Disciplined Style of Life

All that has been said about a summons to faith and a summons to an inclusive community may seem theoretical and pious to those who have seen a congregation in action in Bombay, Berlin, or Podunk. It was easy enough, we might say, for Paul to write this, but what does it have to do with *my* church?

If anyone had a right to despair about the possibilities for good within the Church, it was Paul. He was far more severe in his criticism of the church at Corinth than any modern sociologist so far has dared to be about the Protestant churches in the United States. He accused some of them of being adulterers, homosexuals, drunkards, and thieves and all of them as being gossipers. He saw the shameful side, but he always took hope in the fact that where the Holy Spirit had a chance to work, there would be in the community of Christians a distinctive style of life that would attract others to it. We have said previously that the distinctive quality of the Christian faith is not what men do but what they are willing to trust. Where there is this trust in God's love, it manifests itself in a new life. If the Church is not able to express a quality of life different from the world around it, there would be good grounds to question whether or not it has a mission for the world.

Where Christians Are Not Distinctive

We could never argue that the distinctive element of Christianity is its interracial character. The Muslims claim to be interracial and so do the Communists. In fact, the Muslim record on race is as good if not better than that of the Christian Church. One of Mohammed's wives was a Negress, a point stressed by Muslim missionaries in Africa today. Nor can we say that our distinctiveness is a social welfare program. The Ramkrishna Mission in India is a highly motivated Hindu movement to relieve human suffering. Furthermore, we could hardly claim that the intensity of our devotion is distinctive. The Buddhist can often put us to shame in his discipline of meditation and prayer. Nor can we say it is abstinence from drinking or smoking. Adolf Hitler neither drank nor did he smoke.

Where Christians Are Distinctive

What then is the quality of life, the distinctive quality made possible by fellowship with God whose character we have seen in Jesus Christ?

These four marks of the Christian life are, I believe, distinctive. First, *respect of another's privacy*. At first glance this hardly suggests a distinctive quality of life. But in this technological world the privacy of men and women is being invaded. In Communist societies it is a crude and ruthless invasion. For example, in Communist China the government does not permit anyone the freedom of silence. If the Party becomes suspicious that someone is not in agreement with its policies, that person is asked to give a public speech on the subject in question. Party members then sit back to see what he has to say. If he says the wrong thing, he is immediately in trouble. What they are doing is destroying the last vestiges of a man's privacy. The danger is not confined to the Communist world. In the Western world it is more subtle.

Large corporations are demanding of their executives more and more of their personal lives. The trend in all segments of society towards conformity continues to gain momentum. To belong to the Church should provide something distinctive. Within the Christian community every member should feel secure even if he wants to be different. He is to be accepted for what he is—his race, political views, class are all irrelevant. To imitate the life of Christ is to love people in such a way that we always acknowledge their right to be themselves.

In addition to recognizing and protecting an individual's privacy, the distinctive Christan style of life calls for a rare combination of *tolerance on the one hand and intolerance and anger on the other*. Tolerance is essential. It is the capacity to hold to deep convictions and yet have the capacity to listen to those with other convictions. It is not merely the capacity to hear what they are saying, awaiting only one's chance to speak in turn, but it is to listen genuinely in order to understand. Where intolerance and anger are concerned, the problem is to be angry at the right things. Too many Christians have lost their capacity of "generous hatred" against injustice. It is hard to imagine Jesus smiling as he cleaned out the temple. Christian men and women do not smile when they deal with racial discrimination and corruption in government, or attempt to protect the rights of children and women. Martin Luther King is an illustration of a Christan who feels it a part of his missionary obedience to be angry. "Be angry but do not sin" (Eph. 4:26), enjoins the Scripture, which is to say, "Hate evil, but do not hate the men who do evil."

A third distinctive mark of the Christian life is *anonymous goodness*. It is that quality which can love others but does not draw attention to itself. There are literally thousands upon thousands of people within the churches whose lives testify to this. They are the anonymous men and women who because of their concern for their neighbors here and abroad give of their time and energy to help. This goodness is found among Christian men and women of every land. After Jesus healed the sick, he would say, "Now that you are healed, I ask only one thing: Do not tell others who helped you."

Finally, there is *the quality of joy*. The Gospel of Luke ends with the joyous scene of the disciples in the temple, "And they returned to Jerusalem with great joy, and were continually in the temple blessing God" (Lk. 24:52). Just what did they have to be joyful about? They were an insignificant minority, discredited and, as far as the temple authorities were concerned, leaderless. Yet the picture of this small band of people overcome with joy reminds us as to where *our* joy is to be found. It comes from the fact that Jesus arose from the dead and that his Spirit is now in our midst. Or to put it into Biblical language—"Emmanuel"—"God is with us."

The First Fruits of a New Humanity

In Old Testament times farmers waited with eager anticipation to see the first fruits of the harvest. On the day they were able to bring home that which had ripened first, there was rejoicing. It was a sign that the harvest was near. It was also a sign as to what kind of harvest there would be. When the Scripture speaks of the distinctive style of the Church's life as the "firstfruits" of the new humanity, it is speaking of what was in the mind of Palestinian farmers concerning the coming harvest. A church in one area of the world may be small and weak. It may be in rural areas of Communist China, in Moscow, in an Indian village, on the altiplano of Bolivia, or in East Harlem. But if there is a distinctive style to the life of that congregation, it is a sign to the whole nation that God has already prepared for that people a harvest.

We close this chapter remembering that the Church exists as a summons to faith. It can make this summons only if it is inclusive. It can hope to be listened to only if in its membership it can develop a distinct style of life characterized by reticence, courage, purity, renunciation, discipline, kindness, and joy. All men seek "to belong" to a community of people that knows why it exists, is inclusive, and challenges them to a higher life. It is the claim of the

Christian that for this the Church was created. Yet when we look at our own congregation we cannot but feel shame. Were our congregations and the Christians within them to become more like the vision Paul had for the Christian community the more effective would be our missionary witness.

In an emerging world civilization is there anything more tragic in any part of the world than "to belong" to a local congregation that does not know why it exists, is exclusive in membership, and has no distinctive quality of life in its members?

CHAPTER 7

The Kingdom of God Is
Present and Coming

"He went about doing good . . ." (Acts 10:38).

*I*N the previous two chapters we have considered ways whereby the Christian faith speaks to every man's desire "to be" and "to belong." We have noted the claim of Christians that "to be" in Christ and "to belong" to the Church provides for many a release from the anxiety of meaninglessness characterizing the emerging technological world in which we live.

We have one other question: What does the Christian have to say to every man's desire "to do"? To put the question another way, What does living within the kingdom of God mean to men and women of all nations who want "to do" something that will give purpose to their lives?

The Nature of the Kingdom of God

The message of Jesus concerned the kingdom of God. His first public words were, "The time is fulfilled, and the kingdom of God is at hand; repent, and believe in the gospel" (Mk. 1:15). The startling thing about Jesus' teaching about the kingdom was his insistence that it had already begun. In fact this was his central message. When asked for signs of the kingdom's presence, he either used parables to describe it or referred to his own acts of healing. When, for example, the disciples of John asked him, "Are you he who is to come, or shall we look for another?" (Mt. 11:2-5), Jesus replied, "Tell John what you have seen with your own eyes—the blind see, the deaf hear, the lepers are cleansed, the lame can walk!" This ministry of "doing" has always been recognized by Christians as a sign that the kingdom of God is present in the world. When Luke said of Jesus, "He went about doing good" (Acts 10:38), he was not only summarizing the life of Jesus but also describing in the sharpest possible way the nature of God's rule among men. All this is a reminder that the mission of Christ includes more than verbal preaching. "Not every one who says to me, 'Lord, Lord,' shall enter the kingdom of heaven," said Jesus, "but he who does the will of my Father who is in heaven" (Mt. 7:21). Or again to the question, "Lord, when did we see thee hungry and feed thee, or thirsty and give thee drink?" the King answers, "As you did it to one of the least of these my brethren, you did it to me" (Mt. 25:37, 40).

When we speak of the kingdom of God, or as some would rather call it, "the kingship of God," we must remember that it is not a physical kingdom. If, for example, a news photographer had taken motion pictures of the crucifixion of Christ, there would have been no way to record the presence of God. The film and sound track would have caught the scene and the noise of the crowd and the groans from those dying on the three crosses. But it would not have provided actual physical evidence that God was doing anything particularly significant. When we think of the kingdom of God, it is obvious we must think in another dimension than the purely physical.

The Kingdom Is God's Rule

Although the kingship of God cannot be photographed, it is not imaginary. There is evidence acceptable to any historian to justify the claim of the Christian that God's rule is unmistakable. The death of Hitler and the removal of Stalin's body from a place of honor in Moscow's Red Square are reminders of the fate of evil men. In time their own people will rise up and denounce them.

When we talk about the kingship of God over the world, we are saying that the claims to sovereignty by a nation over her land and her people, or parents over their children, or the Church over her members, or the individual over himself are good only if they do not claim too much.[1] One of the tasks of the Church (as we shall see in a later chapter) is to be the conscience of society. If Christians live under God's rule, they have no alternative but to speak out in protest when they see the nation, or any particular class, or any one race, or any church claiming privileges and powers that belong only to God. The fact that the churches

[1] Roger Lincoln Shinn, *Life, Death, and Destiny* (Philadelphia: The Westminster Press, 1957), pp. 72-73. Copyright 1957 by W. L. Jenkins.

94

have so often failed to do what is expected of a conscience cannot but bring shame upon every Christian.

The Kingdom Comes Quietly

The Christian believes the kingdom of God is now in operation. God rules over all men. Yet the eternal mystery is that this kingdom comes into the world through the quiet, humble events. It comes stealthily. As it pervades the lives of individuals, it does not violate their freedom; for at the center of the kingdom is God's love. This infinite love identifies itself with every man's need, both judging him and inspiring him to forget himself and to give his life to doing good to others. We need to remember that the kingdom is a gift. Christians do not build it. Rather they become channels through which this kingdom of Christ's love is made manifest to the world.

Jesus used parables to describe how this kingdom comes quietly into the affairs of men. The sower, Jesus told his disciples, sows the seed and then goes home to sleep (Mk. 4:26-28). He awakens in the morning to find that the seeds have come through the earth and the harvest is in sight. Jesus used also the Parable of the Leaven. The leaven is small, but it can transform that which is big and lifeless. In Nanking, China, shortly after the Communists came to power in 1949, I attended a morning worship service. We knew there were agents of the Communist Party in the congregation. The Chinese pastor preached on the Parable of the Leaven. He said:

"When Jesus was a small boy, one day he watched his mother make bread. She took the dough in her hands and worked it. Then she picked up in her fingers a small piece of leaven. Jesus asked her what it was. She said, 'Leaven, my son.' She then placed it in the dough, and to the small boy's amazement the dough rose to fill the bowl." The minister then went on to say, "When Jesus grew up to be a man, one day he said to his disciples, 'The Kingdom of God is like a piece of leaven that a woman took and hid in three measures of meal until the whole was leavened.'"

It takes faith to believe that the kingdom of God is being revealed in Communist China. Yet the leaven can work under any circumstances. This has been true in the past and it is true today.

We can see signs of God's kingdom in the lives of people—the most important place to look. Jesus said that his disciples were to be like salt, light, and seed. All these words suggest action, work, and results. In other words, the Christian must witness to the reality of the kingdom of God by what he does. He may not have a chance to witness by his lips. But he will have a chance *to do* something. As long as one lives, one can do good to one's neighbor. Where the act flows out of a relationship with Christ, it can help purify any society. Not only that, it can point to the life of Jesus Christ as the center all men today are seeking.

The Mission to the Jews

But how are we to test ourselves? Perhaps there is no better test for American Christians than to re-examine their approach to the Jews. Judaism is one of the three major religions in the United States. Adherents are found in every community. Many of them are our close and dear friends. It is when we consider the Christian mission to the Jews that some of the implications of living in the kingdom of God are brought into sharp focus for us.

The Problem That Jews Raise for Christians

The novel, *The Last of the Just,* by Andre Schwarz-Bart, is a story of Jewish life. Its first scene is that of the infamous massacre at York on March 11, 1185, when the Archbishop of the day in the name of God proclaimed a campaign against the Jews. Most of the Jews were caught and killed immediately. But a number, with Rabbi Yom Tov Levy, took refuge in a deserted tower, where they were besieged for seven days. On the seventh day the rabbi called together his companions and said to them, "Brethren, God has given us life; let us ourselves give it back to him." So each in turn the Jews drew near to the rabbi, who, after blessing each one with a benediction, thrust a knife into their throats. The final person to receive the benediction and the knife against his throat was the rabbi himself.

Later there grew up a legend among the Jews that God had revealed to the son of the rabbi, who had been miraculously saved, that in each generation there would be born in his family a righteous man who would receive in his own heart the sorrows and sufferings of the whole race. His calling as a Jew would be to accept this suffering upon himself on behalf of all his people.

96

The legend goes that this was to continue down through the centuries as a guarantee that the Jewish people would survive.[2]

The legend has a lesson in it. First of all, it reminds us of the treatment that the Jews have suffered at the hands of Christians. It is a criminal record. The guilt is upon all. Arthur Koestler writes, "The Jews are humanity's exposed nerve," both in terms of their suffering and of their sensitivity to the living God. Some years ago a rabbi commented, "I could believe the Messiah has come if I could only see more clearly the people of the Messiah." This is the most embarrassing statement that a Jew can make concerning Christians.

The legend also reminds us that in spite of all their suffering the Jews survive. Again and again they have stood at the graves of their oppressors. Adolf Hitler is not the first who thought he could crush the Jews. What is the mystery of their survival? What does God plan for them? To the world it is a social problem. But for those who are Christians it is not only a social problem but also a very important theological problem. When Disraeli was asked by Queen Victoria for his proof of the existence of God, he said, "Oh, the Jews, your Majesty."

Similarities between Jews and Christians

We face therefore a problem as to what our attitude as Christians should be. First of all we must see the similarities in Judaism and Christianity: (1) both the Jew and Christian worship the living God of Abraham, Isaac, and Jacob; (2) both confess that this is the one God, our Redeemer, Judge, and King, the One who has created us and who holds us accountable for what we do and what we say; (3) we both believe that God has chosen the people of Israel as his own people to fulfill his purposes; (4) we both believe in a God who acts, a living God, who is involved in the history of the world; (5) we both see man as a creature, a sinner, and we see him as a sinner because he refuses to accept the fact that he is only a man and wants to play always the part of God.

The Point of Difference

The real difference, of course, between the Christian and the Jew is centered in the question as to whether or not Jesus was the Messiah. Was he or was he not the one for whom the Jews waited? The Jew would say, "No." The Christian would say, "Yes."

---

[2] Neill, *Christian Faith and Other Faiths*, p. 20.

Yet both Jew and Christian believe that a kingdom is coming when God will rule. For Christians it will be the final day when Christ returns. For the Jew there is still the vision of the coming Messiah. The question, of course, is whether or not there is a difference between these two understandings of the coming kingdom of God. Paul made a sharp distinction between them. It is Paul who still irritates Jewish thinkers. Martin Buber, the saintly Jewish scholar, feels that Paul is the culprit who corrupted the Christian faith and set it off on its wrong course. But even Paul saw the Jews as a special concern of God. In Romans 9-11 he sees the Jews as an entire people coming to faith in Jesus Christ but only after the Gentiles have heard the message. The question still haunts the Christian. What should we do? Should we consider the Jew in the same category as the Hindu and Muslim, or should we assume they have a special role still to play? And if so, what is it?

Arguments in Favor of Leaving the Jews Alone

Christians today are not in agreement as to what should be the approach to Jewish community. Some feel that the Christian mission should leave the Jews alone. Dr. Reinhold Niebuhr writes, "Practically nothing can purify the symbol of Christ as the image of God in the imagination of the Jew from the taint with which ages of Christian oppression in the name of Christ tainted it." [3]

A second argument in favor of leaving the Jews to themselves is the need for religious harmony in the United States. The point is stressed that we are all Americans with more things in common than in contradiction. Therefore we are encouraged not to stir up the waters. This argument is premised on the assumption that what is really important in American life is not the issues of religious conviction so much as it is the national and cultural patterns which belong to our common tradition. This gives a basis for the argument of some scholars that a national religion already is emerging which is bringing together Jews, Protestants, and Roman Catholics. If this is so, it might be well to ask just what kind of a religion it is that is doing this. Could such a national-centered religion conceivably be Christ-centered?

The third argument in favor of leaving the Jews alone is more

---

[3] Reinhold Niebuhr, *Pious and Secular America* (New York: Charles Scribner's Sons, 1958), p. 108. Copyright 1958 by Reinhold Niebuhr.

persuasive than either of the other two. It is the position of Dr. Will Herberg, a noted Jewish scholar, whose competence to deal with both Christian history and theology is recognized by all.

Dr. Herberg argues that Judaism and Christianity are both part of God's plan. They have, he writes, one covenant, but they participate in two commissions. The commission of the Jews as a people is faithfulness to God. They are not to try to win the world but to continue their historic witness as a unique race obedient to God. Christians, on the other hand, are commissioned to go to all the nations. As they do so, they are to remember, so the argument goes, that the Jews have been given a commission just as meaningful. This position, as one might expect, does not satisfy all Jews or Christians.

A New Approach Is Needed Toward the Jew

It is obvious that the mission to the Jews will not be one primarily of preaching. In fact, to preach Christ to Jews as if they were uncivilized and pagans would be stupid as well as unfair. The test will be not in what Christians say so much as what they do.

The missionary issue as I see it is simple. Are Christians prepared *to do* something or not?

"Doing" would mean first of all confession on the part of Christian men and women that anti-Semitism is still alive within the churches. Its ugly head is seen in many a Christian family. Perhaps one reason for the reluctance to consider Jews as a missionary concern stems from the awareness that anti-Semitism is still alive. It is impossible to conceive of a Christian mission to people where hate is latent.

Along with confession there would be the need to ask forgiveness of the Jews. Crimes against them have too often been committed by Christian people, at times even in the name of Christ. For churches to make a public apology would be humiliating, but it would be a beginning.

Third, there would be needed a determined struggle on the part of Christian people to fight discrimination. This too would not be easy. The Jews seem to be able to take care of themselves. Why should they be set apart for justice? What of the Negroes? And then there are the poor migrants. All this is true. But that does not alter the fact that discrimination against the

Jews is still a serious problem in private clubs, the higher echelons of business, and in housing.

Finally, a new approach would call for respect and appreciation of Judaism and the courageous witness of the Jews to their faith over the centuries. Such an approach would not suggest Christ is not still the one they really seek to know. The Christian can but pray that what he *does* will make possible a more relaxed attitude on the part of the Jew. The Jew needs to take a new look at Jesus Christ. Few of them read the New Testament at all. If they would read it as carefully and thoroughly as the Christians read the Old Testament, it would be a start.

As to the future we cannot say. Was Paul right that the conversion of the Jews would only come after the gospel had been taken to all the nations? Perhaps so, but I find this hard to accept. If Christ is the center of the world, the quicker the Jew sees this on his own the more quickly will come recovery of wholeness and new life.

The Kingdom Is Coming

When we consider the mission of the Christian to the Jew, the New Testament makes it clear that the final outcome rests with God. We cannot answer the question in Paul's mind. The problem of incompleteness is more than that of the Jews. All we have to do is to look within ourselves, within the Church, within the nation, and within the world of nations to realize that this incompleteness is everywhere evident. The kingship of God has begun but it is still incomplete. Christians long for the day when all men will be able to see what they have seen by faith.

The kingdom of God provides a reminder that when history does end, the decisive fact is with God. To believe this is an act of faith. However, for our day it is an important point to stress. To live in such trust in God is a risk, but this very act of trust protects the Christian from panic as he looks at the nuclear arms race. It protects him from the temptation to believe that all evil is in Communism and that we need only to destroy the Russians and a new day will dawn. This does not mean we evade these issues of totalitarianism. But it does mean we are to do our work—to care for our families, to struggle for justice and freedom—leaving the final outcome in God's hands. When that end will come we do not know. Jesus warned against any speculation as to when this would take place. When the disciples asked him when he would restore Israel he replied, "It is not for you to know . . . . But you shall receive power . . . and you shall be my witnesses . . ." (Acts 1:7, 8). In other words, the emphasis should not be on vain speculation as to when this will happen, but on the urgency of going to all men, speaking to them of the mighty acts of God in Jesus Christ.

One theologian has written that the end for which men wait is not like the rugged outline of the Rocky Mountains rising at the edge of the Colorado plateau. Rather it is more as if we were already in the Rocky Mountains, moving from one valley to another. From where we live within the valleys we cannot tell how many ranges are ahead. There may be a million more, or the one in which we move may be the last. In any case we are not to worry about the end but do our work with faithfulness, diligence, and courage.

The World Mission as a Clue to the Meaning of Contemporary History

When we see all men caught in the swift current of technological change, how can we see in perspective the relationship of the world mission of the Church to the political and social movements of our time?

The Book of Revelation provides a dramatic picture of what the early Church had to say in answer to that question. It is the same answer that Christians would give today. We might not use the same imagery. However, the basic idea would be the same.

The Four Horsemen of the Apocalypse

In the sixth chapter of the Book of Revelation there is mention of four horsemen riding through the earth: the crowned rider of Conquest on a white horse; the swordsman of War and Revolution on a bright red horse; the emaciated symbol of Famine on a black horse; and finally Death riding the pale horse of pestilence. It is not easy to apply the language of the Book of Revelation to our present day but it can be done. One author describes the Germany of 1932:

There arose an angelic following out of the heart of Germany, a religious and cultural movement whose angelic power is Nazism. This is a fallen angelic power, and in the presence of it God is doomed;

101

it will destroy itself. But it comes to men with lying and deceitful signs and wonders and with great promises, making the same angelic pretension that was made by Lucifer—the pretension of deity. Therefore it gathers unto itself followers and power. Like all fallen angels who pretend to be God, this power . . . "exalts himself against everything that is called God." It not only is defiant of the true God, but it tyrannizes over every other pretender, and so it is at warfare with the other angelic powers.[4]

In the same way, when we think of the Four Horsemen of the Apocalypse we need not see them as mystical riders, but as powerful movements in contemporary history which we can recognize.

The crowned rider (the first horseman) of *Conquest* we can see in the rise of totalitarian states, the domination of the group over the individual, the dehumanization of man by the machine, the power of the corporation and the union over its members, the "hidden persuaders" of mass communication that mold man's thought and response.

The swordsman (the second horseman) of *War and Revolution* we see in two world wars, the recent fighting in Korea, the killings in Algiers, the racial conflict in the Republic of South Africa, gang warfare, crime and muggings in the big cities, and threatened civil war in the Congo.

The emaciated rider (the third horseman), with a balance in his hand, on the black horse of *Famine* is seen in the appalling poverty of India and China, the slums of the big cities, the poor nations, the migrants, and the millions of children who go to bed every night hungry.

Finally, *Death* (the fourth horseman) on the pale horse comes to the world in cancer, tuberculosis, mental illness, and a legion of other killers. A quick reading of the morning newspaper furnishes evidence that these Four Horsemen of the Apocalypse were out during the night riding through the earth. I recognize that this picture is overdrawn, for it does not indicate adequately the creative factors also at work in the world. There is no question but that these positive forces are strong. We see this in the growing sense of social responsibility that governments of the world feel toward their people; we see it also in the conquest of illiteracy,

4 Albert T. Mollegen, S.T.M., D.D., *Christianity and Modern Man: The Crisis of Secularism* (Indianapolis: The Bobbs-Merrill Company, Inc., 1961), p. 118. Copyright 1961 by Albert T. Mollegen.

typhoid, malaria, and the growing control of mental illness. This and much more is being done. Yet the haunting specter of the Four Horsemen of Conquest, War and Revolution, Famine, and Pestilence remain. In fact their power seems to grow rather than to be weakened.

The Fifth Horseman of the Apocalypse

But the Christian sees something that others do not see. In the nineteenth chapter the Book of Revelation describes this movement as Christ, the King, riding on a white horse, followed by his people who come out of every nation. The militant imagery should not throw us off the central point: the bold claim that the kingdom of God has begun—that Christ moves through the entire world, and behind him follow a community of men and women who share in his mission of reconciliation and love.

If we believe this, it raises many perplexing problems for us. For example, if we are to understand the movements of history in terms of these five horsemen, what about the other religions? Are they not also concerned with the whole world? How does God use them? There are no simple answers, and later we will have to deal with some of the issues involved. Nonetheless, Christians must make a decision about the meaning of their own history as it comes to them in Scripture. If we were to become convinced that the world mission of every Christian congregation in Europe, Asia, Africa, Latin America, and North America was a part of this fifth movement in the world today, what a different understanding we would have of the mission in our communities and to the world!

The idea that the mission of the Church is the clue to the meaning of contemporary history startles us. Yet it is not the first time that this has happened. Arnold Toynbee tells how the Roman Empire built a massive system of roads to preserve the empire. The intricate system of communication did not do what was hoped. In time the empire collapsed. The most lasting achievement of the roads was that they provided travel facilities for Paul, a man the Roman emperors never knew. No one knew it at the time, but Paul's travels were the clue to the meaning of that era of history. He and other Christians were preparing new life that was to break forth at the very time that the old empire was dying. It is our expectation today that the same thing is taking place.

I like J. B. Phillips' translation of Romans: "The whole creation is on tiptoe to see the wonderful sight of the sons of God coming into their own" (Rom. 8:18). It takes faith to live by the expectation that the kingdom of God has begun, and is yet to come. Several years ago a student at Union Theological Seminary in New York in a public meeting asked Dr. John Baillie, the Scottish theologian, if he still believed in the missionary movement. Neither the student nor the crowd were prepared for this reply. He said, "I believe that the Kingdom is at hand. I want people to hear about it." You could have heard a pin drop.

PART THREE

The Task
of
Every Christian

The Mission Field:
A No-Man's Land between Faith
and Unbelief

"The field is the world . . ." (Matthew 13:38).

WE have seen that the 19th century missionary movement, one of the most creative in the entire history of the Church, was characterized by four images:

1. The *mission field,* seen as a rural area where smoke rose in the morning sky from villages that had never heard the gospel;

2. The *missionary,* seen as a white man who went to a distant land to save souls from a perishing world;

3. The word *liberation* meant westernizing Asians, Africans, and the American Indians, for Christianity and Western culture were identified as two sides of the same coin.

4. The restless *explorer* seen as the pioneer of civilization who could not be quieted until every geographical barrier had been crossed.

This understanding gave direction and power to Christian men and women. Even today this understanding determines to no small degree our thinking. However, only a blind man could miss the fact that we live in a world entirely different from that of David Livingstone and Francis Asbury. It should be no surprise, therefore, to find that these images of the last century have lost their capacity to define our situation and to elicit a response from thoughtful men and women struggling with a complex technological age. This does not mean that there was no understanding of God in the last century. There was. But the world has changed, and what was meaningful as an expression of missionary obedience in one generation may not be so for the next. The fundamental nature of the mission as God's offer of reconciliation to man through Jesus Christ does not change, but our ways of expressing it in word, deed, and organization do change.

These recent years have been difficult ones for American Protestantism. In an attempt to adjust to the scientific age many Christians have felt within themselves a spiritual erosion. They have found themselves incapable of expressing their faith in language that is meaningful in a day of astronauts, electronics, television, and telstar. Furthermore, the dream of establishing a Protestant nation has been shattered by the rise of other religious communities, and to compound our problem revolutions have developed in China and Cuba that have raised questions in our minds as to the effectiveness of the traditional missionary enterprise.

In spite of our doubts and fears American Protestants have continued to support missionary efforts at home and abroad. At times these efforts have been like the blind groping in the dark, but the churches have not lost heart. Already we are beginning to see more clearly the direction and form of a new missionary era. Much of the rediscovery is coming through a fresh encounter with the Scriptures. There we have learned again that for the Christian the knowledge of God is that of the triune God who seeks reconciliation with mankind. It is this understanding of God that motivates us to mission. We have seen that although Christians have no more right to speak to Hindus and Buddhists concerning their religion than Hindus and Buddhists have to witness to Christians, all men have not only the right but also the responsibility to share with one another what they consider to be truth.

The Christian claims that Jesus Christ is the Lord who reigns over this new age. Christ, therefore, is the center sought by all men. When this conviction becomes the center of a man's life, he sees as did Paul that the Christian Church exists for a purpose. That purpose expresses itself not only in the message about Jesus but also in a community of people who are inclusive and who possess a distinctive style of life, a quality of goodness, kindness, joy, and courage that sets them apart. Christians say that this quality of life is made possible only by the presence of God's Spirit manifest in his kingdom. It is in this kingdom that Christians claim they are living. To do so is to acknowledge that God rules over the world in love.

We are now ready to look at the future. What are we to do? What is the task of every Christian man and woman? What is the task of every congregation? In this emerging new age is there being revealed to us a fresh understanding of the words "mission field," "missionary," "liberator," and "explorer"? Can we put into these words content capable of describing accurately our situation and of eliciting a response of sacrificial service on the part of Christians the world over?

The Mission Field

If asked the question, "Have you ever been to a mission field?" I presume many would answer "no." This is one illustration of how easy it is still to live in the 19th century missionary world. We have already seen that the image of a mission field in that great century of expansion was of smoke rising from a thousand rural villages in Africa, Asia, or on the frontier of the United States. This was a missionary image of tremendous power. For well over 100 years thousands of men and women died in response to its challenge.

This mental picture of a mission field seems less and less relevant to the urban, technological, complex world in which Christians live today. We hope that in time new images will emerge, as meaningful as were earlier ones. It is too early to say what they will be. Meaningful symbols come only out of involvement and suffering. We may be in a period where such clarity is not possible for us, but we must try to get our bearings and see where we are.

Any image of the mission field today must be related in some way to the common suffering and agony of mankind. We have experienced two devastating world wars and a spate of little ones. The population explosion, the threat of nuclear war, the bitterness of the East-West struggle cast a shadow over all the world. Perhaps we can see the mission field as a no-man's land that lies beneath this shadow. If so, we can compare it to the five-mile no-man's land separating North and South Korea, or the zone of silence between Jordan and Israel, or the wall of separation between East and West Berlin. Such a no-man's land can be compared also to the tension between white and Negro in Mississippi, between Puerto Rican and Negro in New York, or between middle-class suburbanites and slum dwellers.

This picture of no-man's land does not suggest a victorious army marching across all barriers. Such a view of the mission is unrealistic. For instance, there is no way to get into China. Chinese Christians carry the full weight of the mission. In varying degrees this is the situation in other areas as well. In much of the world Christians no longer have an advantageous position.

However, this picture does not for a single moment suggest that

Christians have ended this battle for the minds and hearts of all mankind, nor have we any intention of doing so. On the contrary, the missionary task is to meet people in places where there can be conversation concerning the meaning of man's life and destiny and the meaning of the world.

Any image of the mission field that becomes real to us must include two pictures: that of two persons talking together and that of the world-wide church in conversation with the rest of mankind.

Where Two People Talk

We might say that the first picture has the dimension of depth and the second the dimension of breadth.

The dimension of depth is suggested in two novels by Ignazio Silone. He writes, "The spiritual situation . . . resembles a refugee encampment in no-man's land. . . . What do you think refugees do from morning to night? They spend most of their time telling one another the story of their lives. The stories are anything but amusing, but they tell them to one another, really, in a effort to make themselves understood." [1] And again in another book he writes, "Two men must be alone together, talking softly with many pauses."

Any picture of a mission field must include, first of all, people. To be sure, it includes also social and political movements, but it begins with people trying to communicate with each other:

It is a Christian father talking to his son. So many of the securities of the 1930's are gone, and the young face intellectual questions today their parents never had to face.

It is a theologian and a scientist talking of the world and of God. God has provided for neither the knowledge either would have given if he were God.

It is a doctor talking to his partner, or a farmer to his neighbor, or a housewife to a stranger she has met on a bus, or a student to a professor.

It is a congregation gathering for worship, where the Scripture is read, hymns are sung, and the message given. It is there that every new generation is called out of unfaith to faith, their parents being unable to answer for them.

---

[1] Hamilton, *The New Essence of Christianity*, p. 25. Quoting from "The Choice of Comrades," by Ignazio Silone, collected in the paperback volume *Voices of Dissent* (New York: Grove Press, 1958).

It is a Bishop entering a village in India, being greeted by a handful of Christians. They put garlands around his neck, then the small group proceeds to the center of the village, where the Bishop speaks to Hindus about Christ—the light of the world and the hope of India.

It is two diplomats sitting at a table. The issue is life or death for mankind. How is the Christian diplomat to make his faith in Christ relevant?

Always the mission field is where people talk to each other about human existence. In spite of the fact that today's religious climate is very different from that of the last century, it is still marked by the meeting of men to hear the gospel from the lips of another man. Today Christians are part of a fragmented, divided world. Today the separation of faith and unbelief is more like a no-man's land, a zone of silence, than it is a "lost" village waiting for the missionary to come across the mountains.

This no-man's land is characterized by the hunger of men of all cultures and races to talk about their lives; by the inability of Christians to force their way into the lives of others—they must sit and listen as well as speak; and by the refusal of Christians to withdraw from the battle for the heart and mind of man—in fact, for the first time, churches are in a position to meet the challenge on a world-wide scale.

A World Church

The dimension of breadth in our image of the mission field suggests a conversation not only between persons, but also between communities. The mission field today is a world-wide church confronting a world of unbelief. But how can we see this? Let us imagine an astronaut orbiting the earth. His space ship makes an orbit every ninety minutes. He will be up there for two days. As he orbits the earth, every Christian congregation turns on the lights of its church. All the rest of the world is dark. If this were to be done, the world to the astronaut would look like the Milky Way on a clear summer night. Where he saw a massive cluster of lights he would know he was over North America or Europe; where the lights would be less dense he would believe himself to be over Russia; where they were scattered he would assume he was over Asia, Africa, Latin America, or the islands of the oceans. The important point is that he would see lights everywhere. Should this

111

Businessmen 24,000
Students 10,000
International agencies .... 3,000[1]

Another 30,000 men and women were in part-time work overseas. American military forces overseas number 1,000,000. Wives and
children add to the above list an additional 300,000. The number of
Americans living overseas this year (1963) will be even higher. In
other words, the lives of tens of thousands of Americans, not count-
ing tourists, are related intimately to other people of the earth.
Among that number are many thousands of loyal church people.
Why cannot they be considered missionaries? What constitutes a
missionary life today?

Who Is a Missionary?

In the 19th century the average layman in the church did not
consider himself a missionary. That responsibility rested on a small
elite group professionally set apart for that task. Today we recognize
the inadequacy of such a view. Biblical studies have reminded us
that the Scriptures pay little attention to whether a man is a teacher,
tentmaker, fisherman, farmer, lawyer, preacher, bricklayer, or ma-
chinist. Rather, the Bible makes it clear that the calling of every
Christian is to be a witness, a missionary, and an evangelist.

This has not been understood by the larger part of the Church's
membership. Many laymen have tended to think of their vocation
as making a livelihood. The task of effectively communicating the
Christian message has been left to others. We recognize, therefore,
that the greatest single problem confronting the mission in our day
is the reconversion of Christians to a fuller meaning of the Christian
life. We have rediscovered that at the center of every Christian's
life must be a missionary conviction.

The Mission to Those within the Church

Re-examining the meaning of the word "missionary" calls for
enlisting every Christian in a mission both to those *within* the
Church and those *outside* it.

It is sometimes assumed that there is a difference between the
two. Actually they are part of the same missionary task. Every

---

[1] Harlan Cleveland and Gerard J. Mangone (eds.), *The Art of Overseasmanship:
Americans at Work Abroad* (Syracuse: Syracuse University Press, 1957), p. 27. Copyright 1957 by Syracuse University Press.

year many within the churches lose hope and need help. How easy it is for every Christian, either through stupidity or ignorance, to wander away from the Christian life. Jesus described people as sheep. And so we are. Within every congregation there are those in trouble. The missionary task is world-wide, but it begins within a congregation. The initial missionary task of every Christian is to his fellow-Christian, to the person whom he has at one time or another seen inside his church.

It is not difficult to see the vast sea of human need within a congregation. There are the old, who need comfort and friendship. There are young married couples who need guidance and encouragement. There are children who need instruction and understanding. There are "shut-ins," the sick, the dying, who need hope. Too often we think of the professional minister as the person responsible for meeting these needs. Such an understanding is a reminder that we are still part of the 19th century. The task today is for *every* Christian to see his vocation, his calling from God as a ministry to others. This insight begins within a local congregation as Christians in the name of Christ minister to one another.

There are signs of renewal throughout the churches as small groups have made such missionary concerns come to life.

The Mission to Those Outside the Church

The mission includes responsibility not only for those within the Church but also those outside it. As we have seen, the mission field is everywhere around us. We stand on it every hour of every day. When we recognize this, it is not hard to see the vast mission field at the door of every congregation.

As Christians have tended to think of the minister as the person ministering to those within the Church, they have thought of professional missionaries as those going to those outside. The result is that the local church is seen as a place of fellowship of like-minded people seeking for themselves comfort and assurance. The local congregation has not been a missionary training center preparing men and women to go out into the world to witness effectively to the meaning of their Christian faith within an emerging world civilization. But this we are beginning to see as the task of every church. It is as true for local Christian congregations in Japan, India, China, the Congo, and Brazil as for those in the United States.

Is the Christian Church a Dwindling Minority?

The mobilization of all in the Church to missionary conviction becomes an urgent priority when we see that the Christian community is increasingly a minority. Of all the great religions it is the most strategically poised. It is world-wide, which means that within the emerging new age it has a singular opportunity. But its minority position is more pronounced every year. The rapid rise in the world's population is largely in non-Christian areas. As was mentioned earlier, by the year 2000 it seems likely there will be some 5,000,000,000 non-Christians. The percentage of Christians today is approximately 33 per cent of the total world population. Unless there is a marked change, it will drop by A.D. 2000 to approximately 20 per cent, or 1 out of 5.

Other World Religions Are on Every Street

The question is not only one of numbers. In the years ahead we can expect to find followers of the other great world religions walking the streets in front of our churches. One will not have to travel to India to meet the Hindu or to Burma to meet the Buddhist. They will increasingly be seen in the United States.

Dr. Hendrik Kraemer writes that the encounter with other world religions has just begun. All have their interpretation of the meaning of the new civilization into which mankind has been thrust. All will have a word to say. The crucial problem is to help the layman see that he is the key to the future effectiveness of the mission of the Church at home and abroad. Unless every Christian is alerted and trained to his missionary responsibility, the strategic opportunities in the next half century will not be met.

It is important, therefore, to see the local congregation not as a place where people gather thinking first of their own needs, but as one where they are brought together for training in a missionary task to those outside the Church's life.

Other Religions Fall into Two Types

In the new age we can anticipate two types of response to the Christian message. There will be those who will try to *exclude* from discussion the name of Jesus Christ or the Church or the kingdom of God. This appears to be the mind of the materialist, the Marxist, and the Muslim. They are different in many other respects, but their over-all response to the preaching of the Christian gospel is in this one respect similar.

116

The second type of response will come from the Hindu and the Buddhist. They are concerned not to *exclude* the Christian message, but to *absorb* it. We need to examine both types of response because they have the same long-range objective: to undermine the claim of the Christian that Jesus Christ is the center to which all men must turn if they are to find meaning within the emerging world civilization.

Those Who Would Exclude Jesus Christ

If the local congregation is to be a missionary training center, every person in the congregation must have some knowledge of those whom he will meet outside.

The Materialist

First, there is the materialist. A minister called on a family in an apartment house in London. The daughter opened the door and when she saw the caller's clerical collar said, "We don't need God. We have everything we need." Whereupon the door was shut in the minister's face.

This experience is not limited to London. A materialist (or secularist as some call him) is a person living as if God did not exist. He does not *deny* God. He may even say that he believes in some kind of God. But when he is questioned about what he means by "God," he will give many different answers.

The materialist is a product of the technological age. He sees modern man conquering the world outside and sees no reason why in time he will not be self-sufficient to conquer the world inside as well. There is a nobility about many in this group. They have accepted the natural world as it is and are determined to bring it under man's control. They are often suspicious and skeptical of the Christian's integrity and intelligence in facing the complexity of the modern world. As one said, "You do not have to be stupid to be a Christian, but it helps."

What is the materialist saying? In his book, *The Plague,* Albert Camus writes:

"It comes to this," Tarrou said almost casually; "what interests me is learning how to become a saint!"

"But you don't believe in God!"

117

"Exactly! Can one be a saint without God?—that's the problem, in fact the only problem, I'm up against today." [2]

College students are a special group confronting the challenge of this kind of mind. In the United States 40 per cent of the population of college age are in college. By 1970 it is estimated that there will be 6,000,000 students in American colleges. The same rapid expansion of universities is taking place elsewhere in the world. The Communist sees the strategic importance of the student mind. In recent years Communist China, even with its severe paper shortages, has not slowed down its flow of Communist literature to college students throughout Asia. Christian churches recognize that throughout the world the college campus is today one of the most important mission fields.

No day passes in which Christians do not meet persons who think and act like the girl in the London apartment and the man in Camus' book. Their response to the Christian message is one of indifference. One reason for this is their disillusionment with Christians who they think do not practice what they preach. A second reason is their belief that man has the capacity to save himself.

The Marxist

The second group trying to exclude Christ from any serious consideration in their lives is the Marxist. It is difficult for Americans to deal with the Communist (Marxist) mind. Our democratic thought, our parliamentary and judicial systems are so alien to the Communist way of life that it is almost impossible to find a point of contact. For the Christian this difficulty is compounded by the fact that the Marxist approach to the Christian faith is one of denial and ridicule. The Marxist sees the Christian faith as a monumental lie, a clever fabrication manipulated by those in power to keep quiet the people over whom they rule. The Communists assume that the Christian religion will eventually collapse. They see *their* understanding of history being recognized as the center of the technological age.

What, then, can Christians do? What should be the missionary approach to the Communist? The following suggestions are at least a beginning:

[2] Albert Camus, *The Plague* (New York: Alfred A. Knopf, 1957), pp. 230-231. Copyright 1948 by Stuart Gilbert.

Christians can deepen their personal commitment to God in Christ. Christians can identify themselves more with the underprivileged. Christians can work for change in Communist societies. To do this is to recognize that not all individuals in Russia or China are hard-core Communists. The change will be gradual, but it can be anticipated.

Christians can remember always that Communists are people. After the Communist Party came to power in China, a missionary doctor prepared to operate on a party official. As the nurses were preparing the anesthesia, the doctor said, "I always pray before an operation, asking God's help." As he turned away to say his quiet prayer, he heard the Communist official say in Chinese. "Doctor, pray for me."

The Muslim

The third Christ-exclusionist group are the Muslims. Their response to the Christian gospel is not indifference, as is that of the materialist, or denial and ridicule, that of the Marxist, but that of distortion. Christians experience difficulty in making an effective witness to the Muslim because of the latter's distorted understanding of the Christian message.

Of the approximately 350,000,000 Muslims in the world, the majority are in North Africa, Egypt, Turkey, Iran, Iraq, Pakistan, and Indonesia. However, there are 20,000,000 in China and they are increasing in Africa south of the Sahara. There are about 70,000 in the United States. Thirty years ago seven out of eight Muslims lived under colonial regimes. Now almost all are in independent countries ruled by Muslim leaders. This political situation makes for a relationship very different from that in the last century.

The Muslim poses a special problem for the Christian. The Muslim's spiritual roots are in the Bible. The *Koran,* the Muslim scripture, speaks of Adam, Abraham, and the prophets. The *Koran* teaches also that Jesus Christ was a prophet, and the faithful are instructed that he was born of a virgin. However, there are obvious distortions in other sections of the *Koran.* The Muslim is taught that Jesus announced the coming of Mohammed as the last of the prophets.[3] The Muslim is taught also that Jesus was not crucified, but was rescued in the nick of time by his disciples:

---

[3] Edmund Perry, *The Gospel in Dispute: The Relation of Christian Faith to Other Missionary Faiths* (Garden City, New York: Doubleday & Company, Inc., 1958), pp. 166-167. Copyright 1958 by Edmund Perry.

119

The Jews said boastfully,
"We killed Christ Jesus,
The Son of Mary,
The Apostle of God!"
But they did not kill him,
Nor did they crucify him,
But it was made to appear
That way to them . . .
For of a surety
They did not kill him.
(Sura IV, 157) [4]

It is unthinkable to a Muslim that God could so humiliate himself as to suffer at the hands of men.

How, then, is the Christian to speak to the Muslim? What is the word for Christian American tourists traveling in Egypt or for a Christian in the U. S. Department of State in Indonesia? Probably the most outstanding Christian student of the Muslim world today is Dr. Kenneth Cragg of England. His book, *Sandals at the Mosque,* has a fresh approach to the subject. The title itself says much. To make Christ known, writes Dr. Cragg, means first of all to humble oneself. It means we must remove our sandals and live inside the Muslim's world until we understand more clearly what he believes. Only where this humility of spirit is genuine and constant, Dr. Cragg points out, can we hope that the Muslim will listen to what we have to say about Jesus Christ.

"The Christian does not say," continues Dr. Cragg, "we have the truth; sit down while I tell it to you. But rather, We Christians have found in Jesus Christ the wonder of God as Love. Shall we talk of it together?" [5]

If we see the task only in terms of American Christians speaking to Muslims, we will miss the deeper dimensions of our present situation. Several years ago I asked the Bishop of the 700,000-member Batak Church of Indonesia what he considered the mission of their church in Indonesia, a nation overwhelmingly Muslim.

Through an interpreter, the saintly Bishop said, "We are finding that the Muslim women are buying the gospel tracts from our traveling lay preachers in greater and greater numbers. They hide

---

[4] *Ibid.,* p. 167.
[5] James K. Mathews, *To the End of the Earth: A Study in Luke-Acts on the Life and Mission of the Church* (Nashville, Tennessee: National Methodist Student Movement, 1959), p. 116. Copyright 1959 by The Board of Education of The Methodist Church.

the tracts in the folds of their dresses. Then at night when their menfolk and children are asleep, they crouch down beside a candle. There slowly they read the gospel story." The Bishop added, "If you can see clearly that picture, you have seen our mission in this land."

Several points are noteworthy in the Bishop's comments. First, the attitude of Muslim women is changing. They are no longer satisfied to live in Indonesia as second-class citizens, in a situation in which, for instance, their husbands can divorce them at will. The second point is that the Bishop had in mind as the missionary a non-white man. The person selling the tracts was an Indonesian Christian layman. Finally, the Bishop took it for granted that the responsibility for a mission to the Muslims rests squarely on his church in Indonesia.

Whether the American or the Indonesian Christian speaks to the Muslim, the deepest problem is erasing the distortions concerning Jesus Christ that have prevailed for so many centuries. The Muslim will listen only after he is convinced of the Christian's humility. When that has been established, the Christian can say, "Sir, consider Jesus. We have no other message."

Those Who Would Absorb Jesus

The second type of response to Jesus Christ is seen most clearly in the Hindu and the Buddhist.

The Hindu

The appeal of *Hinduism* is that all religions are the same. Most of the 350,000,000 Hindus in the world live in India, but the influence of their thought is world-wide. The Hindu sees emerging in the new world civilization a Parliament of Religions. He does not believe that the future will belong to any one religion claiming for itself the final revelation, but that the future will see the emergence of a new synthesis of the religions. Dr. Radhakrishnan, the President of India, has presented this point of view with a competent and persuasive pen. Behind his thinking is the conviction that there is no final way, but that all religious truth is relative and tentative. The Hindu will compromise on everything else but not on this basic assumption that all religions are in the final analysis the same.

Once this point of view is accepted, Hinduism shows great creativity. There is the way to God of knowledge, the way to God of love, the way to God of work, and the way to God of psychological exercise. With this point of view it is no surprise to find the Hindu rejecting the claim that Jesus Christ is the one center all men seek. The Hindu does not reject Christianity as a religion of instruction and philosophy. In fact, he welcomes the Christian religion as one of the religions necessary for the world. In some Hindu temples figures of Jesus Christ are placed alongside those of Hindu gods. The Hindu's response to the Christian message is to absorb it, if he can, into the Hindu faith.

The Hindu's argument appeals to many Western minds. Many in our churches, without realizing it, are closer to conversion to Hinduism than they dream. What, then, are Christians to do? The great Bishop Azariah of South India initiated the following practice in the baptism of Hindu converts to Christianity. After the baptism, the Bishop had the new Christian place his hand on his own head and say, "Woe is me if I preach not the gospel." Thus the new Christian was instructed immediately as to his responsibility to be a missionary to his own people. The Church in South India continues to follow this practice.

Hinduism is a world-wide religion. The persuasive appeal of its main theme, "All religions are the same," is heard on the lips of countless thousands throughout the earth. To respond as a Christian is not to try to win by argument. The response is to witness to what one has learned in one's own life about Jesus Christ, an experience confirmed by the whole history of the Christian Church, beginning with the disciples. This is the task of the Christian in India and the Christian in the United States. Neither in India nor in the United States will the strategic witness be that of only the professional ministers; it will be that of laymen as well.

The Buddhist

The other world-wide religion seeking to absorb rather than exclude Christianity is *Buddhism*. The goal of life for the Buddhist is peace. In the kind of world in which we live today, this goal has meaning for many people. Buddhism's great strength is in Ceylon, Burma, Thailand, and Japan. It has strength also in the State of Hawaii.

Buddhism is an affirmation of man's capacity to redeem himself by prayer, fasting, good works, discipline, devotion, and the love of all mankind. In a world of confusion and noise, it seeks peace

122

of mind and escape from the world. It claims to be a religion that can provide an inner peace for mankind which will then make possible peace in the world. In 1956 on the 2,500th anniversary of the birth of Buddha, there was in Ceylon a floodlighted image of Buddha where in big letters were the words, "This is the True Light of the World."

How, then, does the Christian communicate his faith to the Buddhist? The following, as revealed in a dispatch from Taiwan on December 13, 1961, is hardly the right approach:

"A devout Buddhist and a convert to Christianity got into an argument over religion last night. The Buddhist went to the hospital and the Christian to jail. Police said Mr. Lai had struck Mr. Yang on the head with a hammer. Mr. Yang was reported in critical condition."

What is a better way? D. T. Niles, a Methodist in Ceylon, writes: "Ceylon is a land of many religions, and the heart of a religion is never laid more bare than the way it meets death. When faced by death the Buddhist takes refuge in meditating on the nature of death's inevitability. . . . Resignation is the keynote [to his] attitude to death. So that when death visits a home, those that mourn, mourn without restraint. The person who is dead is ended as that person, and the conquest of death is complete." [6] It is, then, on the problem of death that the Christian speaks to the Buddhist.

Shortly before the Communist armies moved into our part of China, I visited a small Chinese village, in which were ten Christians. Their leader was a thirty-year-old doctor. That very morning his wife had, at 28 years of age, died of tuberculosis. The funeral was held in a room crowded with farm people from the village, more interested in seeing me, a foreigner, than sharing in the sorrow of the family. They were all Buddhist. The coffin was open. To my amazement the young doctor preached the funeral sermon. He took from his pockets two eggs.

"In this one," he said, "is only an egg. If you do not use it, it will spoil. But in the other there is a small chicken. It will soon break out and grow!" He then pointed to the body of his wife and said, "You see only her shell. But the life in her has come out and is with Jesus Christ, her Saviour and mine."

The room was silent. The Chinese were no longer looking at

[6] D. T. Niles, *Preaching the Gospel of the Resurrection* (Philadelphia: The Westminster Press, 1954), p. 43.

me. The doctor had touched them all where they lived. Do you remember Luther's comment, "Every man must do his own dying"? Wherever there are people with a message of victory over death, they can be sure of a hearing. The congregation in that village numbered only nine people, but the nine were missionaries, and the young doctor was their spokesman.

Some Are Sent

What we have said so far leaves out an important point. What about the hundreds of missionaries sent by the churches into difficult situations in the United States and throughout the world? Thousands of them labor in the inner city or across racial and linguistic barriers in this country. There are thousands of them overseas. What is the place of the "traditional" missionary in the 20th century? Wherever one travels in the world one will find them.

They are no longer only Westerners. In Sarawak, Borneo, there are Filipino, Indian, Indonesian, Chinese, American, and British missionaries sharing in the missionary task to the Iban people.

Furthermore, the Bible reminds us that there are various gifts of the Spirit. Some individuals, we are told, are to be teachers, others evangelists, other pastors. In the Book of Acts we read that the church at Antioch was told, "Set apart for me Barnabas and Saul for the work to which I have called them" (Acts 13:2).

As we must see the role of every Christian, so must we realize afresh the importance of those sent by the church:

They may be ministering to students in state universities.
They may be working among migrants.
They may be working in difficult racial situations.
They may be sent to the Congo, or to India.
They may be Indians sent to Borneo, or Filipinos to Thailand, or Japanese to Okinawa, or Brazilians to Bolivia or Chinese to the United States.

Wherever they go, those who are sent play a strategic role in the total witness of the Church.

First, they are the *conscience* of the church, reminding all Christians that the central purpose of the church is to be a missionary. To remember an idea is to wrap it up in a person. It is as the local congregation both sends and receives missionaries that this central purpose is remembered.

Second, those who are sent into the world become *links* between churches. They provide the living tie between churches in suburban areas and the inner city, between churches of white persons and those of other races. This is true also throughout the world. Those whom we send to Africa, Latin America, and Asia become links of trust and companionship. This is not an easy role. Methodist churches who have had Asian and African pastors on their staffs for a year or so are learning both the joys and difficulties of receiving missionaries. The younger churches of Asia and Africa learned this long ago. Yet without these living links how can the church be faithful to its summons to be a universal community?

Third, missionaries who are sent are a *sign* of an unfinished task. There is always the temptation to retreat into our own little world, to refuse to face up to the immensity of the unfinished task. When we see the mission field as a no-man's land between faith and unbelief we can also see thousands upon thousands of urban and rural areas where churches are so scattered or so few in number that they are helpless to act without help from their sister churches. If the world were seen as a community of 1,000 people, there would be 350 Christians in the community. In the part of the community where Asians and Africans lived, however, there would be only 35 Christians, 17 of whom would be Protestants; the same ratio would mean 6 Protestants in Latin America. This gives some idea as to the spread of Christian churches, and why some areas are in need of people from beyond their borders to help them.

When we think of missionaries who are sent, three people come to mind: One is Murray Dickson who at 46 was killed in January, 1962, in Bolivia as his car was making its way through the Andes Mountains. Murray Dickson was a man of unusual charm, vision, brains, and drive. His life is a reminder that some of the ablest men and women within the church are those who are sent, and that there is still a high price to pay for missionary service.

Another is Fred McGinnis who for ten years has been in Alaska. He is now President of Alaska Methodist University, but this responsibility came only after years of toil and travel, often under the most trying circumstances. Here is a man of rare ability, prepared, like Murray Dickson, to be sent.

A third person is Dr. Ivy Chou, a young Chinese woman, charming, consecrated, principal of a Methodist theological college in Sarawak, a Ph.D., and recently elected by the World Council of Churches as one of two women on its Executive Committee. When she comes to this country, she comes as one sent by the churches in Asia as a missionary, a reminder that all churches must both receive and send.

A new fact of our time is that this sending and receiving of missionaries is increasingly the concern of churches in all parts of the world. Those who are sent do not claim a higher vocation. They represent all races within the Church. They go to work that is near at hand and work that is distant. They go to share the whole gospel. As they go, they recognize the function given them by the Holy Spirit. They have been set apart for a purpose by churches in Asia, Africa, Latin America, Europe, and North America. They are the conscience of the Church; they are the links between churches; they are, finally, unmistakable signs that the missionary task is still unfinished.

There is no easy way to resolve what appears at first to be a paradox: "all must go . . . but some are sent." Both statements are true. Emerging symbols of the missionary include both ideas. The New Testament speaks of a diversity of gifts but only *one* missionary responsibility, which is on every member. Furthermore, if contemporary history is teaching us any lesson, it is this:

The challenges confronting the churches are so massive, so complex, so critical that anything less than the response of the whole membership will not be adequate to meet them. Every Christian must see himself or herself as a missionary of Jesus Christ confronting people in the no-man's land between faith and unbelief.

CHAPTER 10

The Liberator:
Every Church a Servant

"The sabbath was made for man, not man for the sabbath . . ."
(Mark 2:27).

*W*E have seen that one of the roles played by the missionary of the 19th century was that of liberator. It would be impossible to understand the life of David Livingstone without recognizing his determination to end the slave trade in Africa. What was true of David Livingstone was true of thousands of others. When I was a boy, my father, at the risk of his life, participated in a campaign to end girl slavery in Southern China. One can never underestimate the liberating influence that has come out of the Christian Church.

To be sure, David Livingstone identified uncritically the Christian gospel with the Westernization of the world. Such an identification might be excusable for the day in which he lived, but it is inexcusable today.

Whatever else might be said of present-day missionary objectives, it is quite clear that the Westernization of the world is not one.

What, then, is the liberating role of the church in the contemporary world?

It is the conviction of this writer that one of our critical missionary concerns is the responsibility of "humanizing" every part of society. By this I mean that the care and protection of man is one of the primary tasks of the Christian mission.

The Amsterdam Assembly of the World Council of Churches put it in these words:

"Man must never be made a mere means for political or economic ends. Man is not made for the State but the State for man. Man is not made for production, but production for man." [1]

[1] World Council of Churches, *Man's Disorder and God's Design: The Amsterdam Assembly Series,* Volume III, "The Church and the Disorder of Society" (New York: Harper & Row, Publishers, Inc., 1949), p. 192.

To explore what this means we need to look at the task of the Christian when confronting the nation-state, race, urbanization, automation, and human misery.

The Christian Within the Nation-State

The task of every Christian and every local congregation in the nation is twofold. First of all, Christians have a prophetic function. They are to be the conscience in the community. When there is injustice, against an individual or a group, Christians should be the first ones to speak out against it. The second function of the Christian is that of a servant. His task is to provide within his own life and the life of his local congregation an example of honest, faithful, and diligent service to the whole community.

This is an easy thing to say. It is a hard thing to practice. One reason why it is hard to practice is the theological conservatism that teaches Christians that they should not meddle in the affairs of the world. Many Christians recognize now that this attitude is wrong. It is Biblically wrong. One cannot study the lives of the Old Testament prophets and the life of Jesus without recognizing that the prophets and Jesus were not afraid to speak out against injustice. Fortunately, there has come a changed attitude among Christians. Social action we see now not as a peripheral part of the Church's mission but as something essential. There is a need for society to change constantly if it is to be more in harmony with the kingdom of God. By this I do not suggest that men can build the kingdom of God. They cannot. Only God can establish his kingdom. However, I do hold that men are responsible to judge and criticize the society in which they live in terms of what that society does to provide the conditions that make the fullest life possible for every man.

But when we say that our task is that of a conscience and a servant, what specifically is involved?

The Church as a Conscience

As the conscience within the nation, Christians must watch for three things. First of all, they should keep an eye on their national leaders. If these leaders begin to claim for themselves or the state absolute authority, then the time has come for Christians to protest. The nation-state is not God; it is not morally autonomous. As I write, the Anglican Bishop of Ghana has been forced to leave that country. He challenged President Nkrumah's claim to be above criticism. If German Christians had done this in the early 1930's, Adolf Hitler might never have cut his ghastly path of blood through the Jewish population of Europe.

Not only must Christians watch their national leaders, they must be alert also to the first signs of persecution against minority groups. We need to be reminded that there was no smile on the face of Jesus when he cleaned out the temple. The struggle to protect minority groups is never easy.

Finally, the Christian conscience recognizes that religious freedom is basic to all other freedoms. Where a man or a woman does not have a right to worship God in freedom, then fundamental issues of justice are at stake. It is for this reason that Protestants cannot rest until there is religious freedom in Spain. Furthermore, in Muslim and Hindu countries where this freedom is denied, the Christian must have the courage to speak.

All this is but another way of saying that Christians should not be afraid to intervene in the affairs of the world. It is the Christian gospel that has helped bring about the revolutionary changes of our day. The tragedy is that once these hungers for freedom, the better life, and equality have been released, Christians have tended to stand back as if they had nothing to do with it.

This is a special warning to Americans. The warning is that the judgment may not be far off unless Americans are able to identify themselves more effectively with the needs of Asia, Africa, and Latin America. It is always a shock to discover what the Old and New Testaments say about God's dealing with the prosperous who are unwilling to assume responsibility for others. The Old Testament prophets repeatedly announce judgment upon them. The Beatitudes of Jesus give special attention not to the prosperous but to the poor in spirit and the persecuted. The death of Christ on the cross is a reminder that God comes to the world through that which is lowly. When we speak of God identifying himself with the underprivileged, the poor, the needy, we do not mean that all revolutionary change is good. It is not. But it does mean that the revolution of our time towards freedom, a better life, and greater equality among men is tied to the requirements of Christian justice. If the Bible is clear at any one point, it is this. God is concerned with those at the bottom of the social pyramid. Because this is so, the Christian conscience keeps the Christian committed to meeting their needs. Never was there a greater challenge for Christians to

129

help initiate in every nation a massive strategy of service and care for those at the bottom of the pyramid—the illiterate, the impoverished peasants, the exploited industrial worker.

The Church as Servant

As a servant within the nation every Christian is to provide an example of integrity, self-sacrifice, and hard work. One of the contemporary problems is that many Christians do not know whom they are to serve. They fail to see that Christ can only transform society through his disciples. It is only when Christians themselves are redirected, reinvigorated, regenerated that they can hope to provide the salt and leaven that can remake the community.

No man has played a more creative role in rethinking of the mission of the Church than George MacLeod. His vision and energy made possible the Iona Community in Scotland. He has attempted to develop a missionary center relevant for a highly industrialized Scotland and England. MacLeod writes:

Bernanos, the French, loving critic of the Church, has a daring picture of the Bride of Christ as the farmer's wife! He visits the farm and finds all in disarray: there are the workers to be given breakfast at five, the children to be got up and fed for school, the farmer returning around 9 for his own full breakfast, the milk pails to be scalded, the big midday dinner, the children returning hungry at 6, the darning to be done, the letter to be written to the absent son, and the early bed: to be ready for it to start again the next day at 5. The kitchen and the farmyard seem in perpetual disarray. Could it not be neater? he asks. . . . Later, he returns to the same farm. The children are crying. The farmer is broken. The workers are querulous. The yard is derelict. The kitchen is chaotic. Why? Because the farmer's wife has died.[2]

In this image of a faithful, careful, hardworking and devoted farmer's wife we see, says Mr. MacLeod, the Church. Its role is that of a servant. It is by no means perfect. But it "keeps God's world from complete disaster."[3]

What is greater, asked Jesus, the one who sits at a table or the one who serves? Plato would have said the one who sits at the table. Jesus says the servant (Lk. 22:27). That, he said, was his own role. In the Fourth Gospel the story of Jesus washing the feet

---

[2] George F. MacLeod, *Only One Way Left* (Glasgow: Iona Community, Community House, 1956), p. 94.
[3] *Ibid.*, p. 94.

of his disciples takes the place of the Last Supper. This is an indication of how important the writer of that gospel considered the incident. When a Japanese student was asked why he became a Christian, he replied: "It was the picture of Jesus kneeling before his disciples washing their feet that changed my life."

It is not difficult to see what servanthood specifically requires.

It is estimated that in Asia some five million men and women must be trained in the next few years. This is a staggering task. The same problem confronts the nations of Africa and Latin America. Such a training program will largely be carried forward by the state. However, voluntary agencies will have their part to play. The development of the Congo Polytechnic Institute in the Congo is one illustration. With independence it became evident that thousands of trained leaders would be needed. In the past the leadership had been overwhelmingly Belgian. But how was this training of technicians, civil servants, typists, accountants, engineers, nurses, and others to be made possible? As a service to the new nation, the Christian churches are determined to find ways to train some 17,000 civil servants in these needed tasks.

In Northern Rhodesia 2,000 trained Africans are needed in the next two years. The problem of Christian motivation is to help them see the need to go to those at the bottom and serve them. The same would be true in Puerto Rico and the new States of Alaska and Hawaii.

The same responsibility confronts Christians in the United States. There are neglected people that the public social welfare agencies cannot adequately help. Christians can still serve such special groups as the handicapped, the old, unwed mothers, the migrants, the mentally retarded, the spastics, and the mentally disturbed.

Some Americans seem to believe that it is possible to be a Christian only in a democratic, capitalistic society. This is simply not true. Jesus did not live in such a society. Neither did Augustine, Francis of Assisi, or Martin Luther. The Church can survive and be effective in every kind of social system. This does not suggest that it can be equally effective in any system. It is obvious that in a free society it will have much more opportunity. Yet the Church can survive and witness in every society. Almost all the younger churches are living in socialist welfare states. They will face some problems not confronted by Protestants in the United States.

It is important, therefore, to keep in mind that there are methods of providing checks and balances within a social system other than the two-party system or Roberts' *Rules of Order*. Christian communities in every part of the world cannot abdicate their role as a conscience and a servant, but how they will enact this role will vary. No one pattern of society is to be identified with the kingdom of God.

The Church's Task Among the World of Nations

All Christians live not only within their own nation, but also in a world that includes all nations. Those who live in the West have had a longer experience with nation-states. They have learned that national loyalties can be too narrow, hatreds too intense, memories too long. They recognize that it is their nations that possess the power that can destroy mankind. "Depend on it," wrote Dr. Johnson, "when a man knows he is going to be hanged in a fortnight, it concentrates his mind wonderfully." [4]

It is not only Christians who see the inadequacies of nation-states. The technologist, whatever his citizenship, sees emerging a technologically united world. The military mind, the business mind, the space mind have already seen that many of the old lines of nation-states are no longer relevant to deal with the pressing problems of the new age.

The Communist mind is also aware of this danger of excessive nationalism. It sees the world divided not into some ninety nations, but into three worlds—the Communist world, the capitalist world, and the neutralist world.

We are discovering that the mission of the Church calls us to be a conscience and a servant not only *within* the nation-states but also *among* them. When the nation-states make claims of absolute authority, or persecute minorities within their borders, or do not grant religious freedom, then the churches together must speak. In the years ahead the political structures of the nation-states will change. The emerging world civilization will make this inevitable. The nation-states have survived 300 years, but no structures are permanent in God's eyes. If the axe of God is cutting at the root of the nation-state we should be aware of it. There are many issues: disarmament, world government, joint space efforts of East and West, the sharing of the West's technological know-how with Asia, Africa and Latin America.

---

[4] Galbraith, *The Affluent Society*, p. 75.

We have looked at the mission of the Church within the nation and among the nations. We need to focus sharply on four different areas within the life of every nation.

Race

Here is an issue broader than the tension between the Negro and the white person in the United States. On a world scale the issue includes the tension between the Malay, the Indonesian, the Filipino, and the Chinese in Southeast Asia; the various African tribes in Africa; the Spanish-bred white people and the Indian-bred brown people of Latin America.

When the Jews were being killed by the thousands in Germany, a German minister, later executed by the Nazis, wrote, "Only he who cries out for the Jews has a right to sing the Gregorian chant." His words are applicable to every racial situation.

In an earlier chapter of this book, was an account of Willie, the Negro boy who was restrained by his minister from getting into a "gang rumble" with razor blades. In another section of his book, *Light the Dark Streets,* the author refers again to Willie:

Willie, I know that I never fully will understand you. I cannot penetrate the pain so often on your face. . . . Once you said to me that you never walk down Henry Street without feeling that the white people passing by are looking upon you with distrust and pity. . . . Sure, I know why you and Bob and Chris and the others banded together; you almost had to form a club. But way inside I know that I cannot understand. . . . Another time I sent you for a job which had been arranged on the telephone. You returned later to say that you were the first to arrive but that the man had hired the boy next in line, a white boy. I tried to explain that perhaps the second boy had the right qualifications and that you may have not. You said that no questions had been asked of either of you by the boss. . . . Do you remember how I stammered and then dropped my gaze from you? Do you remember, Willie, the long silence, my attempt to tell you how I felt? And you did not understand me!" [5]

It is only when we see the hurt on a person's face that the demonic nature of prejudice comes to us. Prejudice is a cancerous growth in the mind that destroys reason and love. The task of every Christian is to expose prejudice in himself and in others. It is a de-

---

[5] Myers, *Light the Dark Streets,* pp. 34-35.

nial of God's fatherhood and his sovereignty over the world. It is a denial of Christ's teaching.

The test comes when a Negro family moves onto a street in a white suburban area; or a Chinese girl marries an Indian in Malaya; or a white Afrikaner has to decide whether to help a Bantu African accused of breaking the apartheid laws.

Alan Booth says that the man caught in a storm who keeps his head and judges soundly the effects of the wind and water, disposing his resources to meet them, is much more useful than the person whom fear withers or heroics tempts to dramatic action.[6] The same is true in racial tension. When a Negro moves onto the street, it is no time for either fear or heroics but for hard work in helping the community face up to the requirements of justice and then to welcome the Negro family as a visible witness of Christian love. When we face issues of this kind, we have an opportunity to learn something about vicarious suffering. If the reader doubts this, test it in your own neighborhood when you have the chance.

The Urban Octopus

Another problem confronting Christians is the cities. Truman Douglass writes, "There are three great areas of our world which the churches have not really penetrated. They are: Hinduism, Islam, and the culture of modern cities."[7] The urban areas of the world have become a magnet in every nation. Already the city of Tokyo has a larger population than the entire state of Texas. The flow of people from rural areas into the cities continues. It is estimated that within the next 20 or 30 years we may see cities of 20 million and conceivably later, of 50 million. Some estimate that by 1980 the USA will be broken down into fourteen "strip cities" comprising 60 per cent of the population.

The dilemma of the Protestant in the United States is that his orientation is rural. He has not been prepared for the urban area in which he now finds himself. The Roman Catholic Church has had an advantage. Its whole life in the United States has been city-centered because most of its people have been industrial workers.

How then can churches in Tokyo, London, Los Angeles, and the other great cities of the world be more effective in caring for people? George Webber writes of an experience in the East

---

[6] Alan Booth, *Christians and Power Politics* (London: SCM Press Ltd., 1961), p. 15. Copyright 1961 by SCM Press Ltd.
[7] See Marty, *The New Shape of American Religion*, p. 104.

Harlem Protestant Parish. On the street parish members found a man hit by a car. They called an ambulance, which did not get there for over an hour. There were two missionary problems: first, to get the particular individual to the hospital; second, to find out why the ambulance took over an hour. This called for conversation with both hospital and police authorities.

The role of "humanizing" servant in an urban community calls for aggressive action. The East Harlem Protestant Parish was accepted as part of the community when it became known that its concern for people involved both talk and action.

Automation

Related to the problem of the big cities is automation. In the United States nowhere has automation affected life more than on the farms.

At 5:30 one frosty Indiana morning last week, Farmer Warren North, 45, rolled out of bed to get at his chores. After a hearty breakfast . . . he left his twelve-room white frame and fieldstone house, walked briskly to the barnyard. In the early morning mist the low-lying white barn, surmounted by five giant blue-black silos, rode the frozen prairie like an ocean liner. Like a rumble of surf came the hungry bellowing of 400 whitefaced Herefords and the grunting of 500 Hampshire hogs, waiting at row on row of troughs to be fed. In the barn North stepped up to an instrument panel as intricate as a ship's, began pushing buttons and pulling switches. All around, the barn came to vibrant life. From one silo dropped ground corn, from another silage, from a third shelled corn.

By pushing other buttons, Farmer North shot in supplementary vitamins, mineral and hormone nutrients. Then he cut in the big noisemaker. In a channel in front of the silos a snakelike auger began to turn. As it writhed, it propelled the feed up a steep incline and sent it tumbling out through a conduit that passed directly over 330 feet of feed troughs. At regular intervals, trap doors automatically distributed the individual animal's feed. When all the animals on one side of a trough had been fed, the traps changed position, shunted feed to the animals waiting on the other side.

Ten minutes later, Farmer North was through with a job that would have taken five men half a day working with buckets and pitchforks. He was ready to indulge in his hobby. He returned to his farmhouse and poured himself another cup of coffee.[8]

---

[8] Robert W. Spike, *Safe in Bondage: An Appraisal of the Church's Mission to America* (New York: Friendship Press, 1960), pp. 53-54. Copyright 1960 by Friendship Press, Inc. Taken from *Time* (March 9, 1959). Copyright 1959 by Time, Inc.

The same impact has been felt in the cities. A vice-president of the Ford Foundation, W. H. Ferry, writes that we are moving toward a crisis in the American economy, the crisis of abundance.[9] This is the crisis of having been so successful with production that we cannot adequately consume what we have produced. Since 1946 we have seen the "second industrial revolution" in the United States. Each year 1,250,000 new people arrive on the labor market, and an additional 1,250,000 are dropped from the existing market because of automation. Ferry's prediction is that eventually we will have to rethink our entire economy. John Kenneth Galbraith, the United States Ambassador to India, has been saying much the same thing. We can disagree with his facts and recommendations, but who would suggest that automation does not raise new issues for Christians concerned about the needs of man. I asked a Methodist minister what he considered the three greatest problems facing his congregation. The three problems he mentioned were all related to automation's impact on American life. How are people to use creatively their leisure time? What are people to do who retire at 60 and live to be 75? What is the responsibility of the government to be when confronted with an economy of abundance? These are all missionary questions.

Human Misery

The picture of Farmer North is not the typical one even in the United States, let alone the rest of the world. What he does every morning is a picture of what is coming. Yet in great sections of the world the suffering continues. There are the hungry, the sick, the illiterate. Every morning at four in the city of Hong Kong children of five and six congregate to catch the beetles that fly around the lights. What they catch will be taken to the market in the morning to sell for a few pennies.

Such stories are before us every day. The problem is to remain sensitive to the fact that those who suffer are not Chinese, Africans, or Indians, but humans. There is also the need to be ready to meet emergencies when they arise. After the Chile earthquake in 1960, in a few days plans to send relief were complete. Some years ago in India there was a serious flood. Through the night a relief team of Church World Service made its way to the stricken area. When

---

[9] W. H. Ferry, *Caught on the Horn of Plenty* in Bulletin of the Fund for the Republic (January 1962).

they arrived, the comment from one of the elders of the area was not a word of thanks, but rather, "We knew you would come!" This is a reminder of what is expected of a servant. A servant does not expect gratitude. A servant is one under authority who is expected to serve.

The task of every church, every congregation in the contemporary world, is to become a servant within the nation and among the nations. It is inconceivable to think of the task as that of Westernization. The need for that which liberates man is still that for which the world waits. Years ago Louis Pasteur was voted the most distinguished of all Frenchmen. When he was a boy his schoolteacher wrote of him, "He is the meekest, smallest, and least promising pupil of my class." At seventy, when he was too weak to go to the celebration in his honor, his son read his message: "The future will belong not to the conquerors but to the saviors of mankind." [10] Perhaps the image we need for our day is that of Christian men and women performing two functions in society—that of conscience, protecting man from any power that claims final authority over him and that of a servant, setting an example of a life that is one of honest, diligent, painstaking service toward the community in which we live.

The role of servanthood is the task of every Christian. To see this is to find powerful new images for our day. This image of a servant community is Biblically accurate and historically relevant. There is every reason to believe it can elicit a response of dedication and commitment as deep as those of the last century.

[10] Harry Emerson Fosdick, *Dear Mr. Brown* (New York: Harper & Row, Publishers, Inc., 1961), p. 100. Copyright 1961 by Harry Emerson Fosdick.

The Explorer:
The Churches Regroup for Expedition

"That they may all be one . . . so that the world may believe . . ."
(John 17:21).

THE mark of a great age is risk. In the fifteenth century Columbus and Vasco da Gama accepted the risk of challenging the high seas, initiating an age of expansion. In the sixteenth century Martin Luther, with equal courage, challenged Rome, and the Reformation was born. In the eighteenth century our American forefathers, against the advice of many of the ablest thinkers of the day, took the risk and put into practice a new form of government. In the nineteenth century, against almost insurmountable difficulty, missionaries challenged the unexplored map of the world.

Willingness to accept risk as the mark of a great age is as challenging today as in the past. The tension of watching a missile, with a man inside the capsule, rising from a launching pad is almost unbearable. All who watch are aware of the implications if anything goes wrong. Yet the flights continue, and within a few years efforts will be made to go to the moon. The same willingness to risk untried ways is evident in the thinking of our political, economic, and scientific leaders. Our survival as a race now depends on our willingness to risk new ways of working together with other nations.

It should be no surprise, then, to learn that denominations are involved in the same perplexities and risks as they look at their own lives. Shortly after the organization of the provisional World Council of Churches in 1938, Dr. W. A. Visser 't Hooft, the General Secretary, compared its early years to that of a sea expedition as risky as that of Columbus. In a frail ship, he wrote, with an inexperienced crew speaking many different languages, disagreeing on the meaning of the Church, the Lord's supper, politics, culture and theology, sailed forth the World Council in 1938 into one of

139

the worst storms of history, not knowing where it was going but holding firmly to the Cross which reminded it of God's victory over man.

The coming together of the denominations has been a risky venture, but we live in a day of risk, and there is more to come. It would be wrong to read the last forty years of the churches' coming together in any other but missionary language. We are witnessing today a world-wide regrouping of churches as we prepare for a missionary expedition into the next century.

It is dangerous to make predictions about the future. Those I am about to make may all prove to be wrong. However, we need as the navigator not only to get a reading as to where we are but to plot on the map where we think we are heading. I believe that there are eight developments deserving our careful study:

1. *In spite of resources we will marshal for the missionary outreach, in the years ahead the percentage of Christians in the total world population is likely to drop.* Too many babies are being born in Asia, Africa, and Latin America in non-Christian families. In fact, if a bold effort is not made to extend the Christian faith on a world-wide scale, fifty years from now the position of the Christian churches may have been seriously altered. In all probability, as we have already seen, the non-Christian population by A.D. 2000 will be somewhere around 5 billion people.

2. *Nowhere in the world will there be a greater test of the creativity and willingness of the Church to try new ways than in the mission to the United States.* The challenge is to provide a "humanizing" influence as the nation deals with the problems of automation, urbanization, race, and world responsibility. The release of the creative powers of the individual within a rapidly changing mass society is a missionary challenge as great as any in the past. If this is not possible within our mission to the United States, one wonders how relevant will be our missionary movement to the world beyond.

3. *In the immediate future nation-states will remain the political structure in which churches must live.* This will call for rethinking as to the structures of church life. I believe that churches in every nation will need to be self-governing and autonomous. This will be true particularly in Asia, Africa, and Latin America. When we remember our own history, we will see the situation now confronting many younger churches.

140

During the Revolutionary War in 1776 the Methodists were severely criticized as being an "alien" church. At that time the American Methodists were still related to John Wesley in England and considered a society within the Church of England. During the war, when Barrat's chapel in Delaware was being built, an observer reflected popular sentiment when he remarked, "It's no use putting up so large a dwelling for Methodists, for after the war a corncrib will hold them all."[1] Following independence, however, the Methodists made a major decision about their future. They severed their ties with both John Wesley and the Church of England and became a self-governing autonomous church. Within seventy-five years the Methodist Church was to be the largest Protestant church in the nation. This is a lesson for all of us as we look at Methodist-related churches throughout the world.

4. *The rise and influence of Christian laymen will be felt throughout the world*. When Ignatius, the early church father, wrote, "The Church consists of the Bishop and his clergy," he was reflecting the temptation of clericalism, which has been with us ever since. As a part of this lay movement will be the growing influence of women. There are some who argue rightly that the greatest worldwide cultural change of the last 150 years is the emancipation of women. We are on the threshold of trying to see what this means within the life of churches throughout the world.

5. *The number of foreign missionaries will continue to rise*. The number now hovers around the 42,000 mark. There would be no reason why churches throughout the world could not support 75,000 in strategic places. As this number increases, the challenge will be to make sure that a greater and greater percentage are Latin Americans, Asians, Europeans, and Africans. At the moment two out of three are North Americans.

6. *The World Council of Churches and regional ecumenical councils will grow in influence, simply because that is what we will want and what self-governing churches in Asia and Africa will want.*

7. *The financial income of the church within the United States for missionary purposes both within the country and throughout the world may double*. The problem is how to plan now for the wisest use of these funds in terms of the whole church in the whole world.

8. *There will be more and more conversations with the Roman*

---

[1] Hudson, *American Protestantism*, p. 57.

Catholic Church. The same will be true with Fundamentalist groups. In a day such as the one into which we are moving, Christians must talk to each other in new ways. The events of history demand it. For example, in Ceylon several years ago discussion in the churches towards closer working ties had slowed down. One Ceylonese Christian remarked, "One more anti-Christian riot, and the discussions will start again." And they did! Not only does the external world push us in this direction, more important still is the recovery of the oneness in Christ of all Christians.

The Regrouping of the Churches and American Denominationalism

It is hazardous to approach so complex a subject in one section of one chapter. No one is certain what the next steps should be, but there is growing awareness that we need to be open-minded and relaxed as we think through the alternatives before us. *Some motives* in the direction of the regrouping of the churches, we can see, *are unproductive.* One is the motive to create a big church for the sake of having *power.* A second unproductive motive is *anti-Roman Catholicism.* That which is conceived in fear and envy can only produce fear and envy within the new creation. A third sterile motive is *tolerance.* If denominations gloss over their theological and structural differences, confusion is certain to follow. The emerging new church structures can come only as the denominations *go through* their differences rather than trying *to skirt around* them. Paul warned against insipid Christians that hold nothing to be important for themselves and expect the same of others. But Paul also wrote to the Corinthians that if their Christian witness was divided it would not be effective (I Cor. 1:11-14).

The Valid Motive

One man has compared the movement of the churches toward greater unity to a circle. On the circumference are the denominations. At the center of the circle is Jesus Christ. Each of the denominations is desperately trying to get closer to Christ. They find, however, that they cannot get closer to Christ without getting closer to each other. This is another way of saying that unity within the churches comes out of faith. It is given to us by God. Christ gives you to your Presbyterian neighbor as he also gives your Presbyterian neighbor to you. Christians have never been able to read the words, "Holy Father, keep them in thy name, which thou hast given me, that they may be one, even as we are one," without a sense of shame at the division so evident in the churches today.

The Visible Witness

As we share in this regrouping of the churches as part of missionary planning for the future, we ask ourselves what this will mean in concrete terms. At this time we simply cannot say. Two things, however, seem clear.

First of all, there must be a visible witness of Christians coming together to talk. When we see Methodists, Presbyterians, Episcopalians, and representatives of the United Church of Christ sitting together around a table considering merger, it is a visible witness. It does not mean that a decision has been reached, but the witness is there. Methodists are both speaking and listening. Episcopalians take the Lord's Supper more seriously than do Methodists. Let's face it. It's true. Presbyterians have shown more sustained concern for Bible study. Congregationalists have been more determined to retain the integrity of the separate congregation. And Methodists have *their* tradition to share. They can be proud of their insistence on freedom in theological expression, the demands of personal discipline, and the requirements of social justice. One would hope that laymen as well as ministers will become aware of the issues involved. Individual Christians should ask, What can I do specifically in my own congregation? What does the Bible say about Christian unity? Can we reconcile the Episcopal and non-Episcopal forms of worship? What is the influence of "social class" on our churches? How is race involved in the problem of denominational division? How can we avert the dangers of a monolithic church?

Second, Christians must come together not only to talk, but to work together. An example is the new Church Center across from the United Nations, put up by Methodist money, but under the direction of an interdenominational board. It is inconceivable to think of Christian mission responsibility in the United Nations as being that of only one denomination. What is true concerning the United Nations is true in many other areas of the Church's life as it confronts the modern world.

Older and Younger Churches

What has been said about the relationship between denominations within the United States can be said of the relationship between the

143

younger churches of Latin America, Asia, and Africa, and the churches in the United States. In an earlier day Western churches looked upon these younger churches as their private "mission fields" around the world. Now we see them as brother churches, co-laborers in the missionary task. The relationship at times is strained, and when this happens the fault is on both sides. American churches sometimes are unwilling to let go of financial control when they should. Furthermore, we have not done as much as we should to help them see their relationship to the world church, and our lives have been free neither of arrogant insistence that the American way of doing things is the right way nor of ignorance of the richness and enduring contributions of Asian, African, and Latin American culture.

At the same time, strained relationships have resulted partly from the actions of the younger churches. It is not true of them all, but some younger churches have been tempted to live unto themselves rather than to reach out aggressively into new areas. At times they have not handled the problems of missionaries living in their midst with the understanding that they would want given them in the same situation. Furthermore, they have been inclined to forget that the money that reaches them comes from sacrificial giving on the part of thousands of Christian people who, when they give, do so at a personal cost.

Today there is a frankness that is a sign of maturity. The younger churches are no longer junior partners, but full partners with the churches of the West. There is no longer a relationship of father and son, but that of brother and brother. Brothers do not always agree, but their relationship is one of complete equality. Therefore, we are having to look more carefully at our past procedures which came out of a period of father-son relationship and adjust these procedures to that of a brother-brother relationship.

This has demanded a restudy of the words *success, stewardship,* and *sacrifice.*

Success

If we think of success in mission as growth in numbers and the development of a church organization like our own, we may be in for disappointments. There will be many areas where the Church will grow, but in the inner city and among Muslims and even the Jews, it will be slow going. The same will be true of organization.

In general, Western church organization is exceedingly costly, clerically dominated, and top heavy. When David went forth to battle Goliath, he was offered Saul's armor. He finally refused to wear it. One of the perplexing problems faced by younger churches as they regroup is to decide how much of Saul's armor they need. Success, then, must not be interpreted in terms of how closely younger churches imitate older churches in their organizational patterns.

Stewardship

The problem American churchmen face is their affluence. How are we to understand our high standard of living? There is general agreement that we are the wealthiest people in the world, but not all would agree as to why this is so. Some non-Americans argue that it is because we are imperialist, living off the rest of the world. This is neither true to the facts nor fair to Americans. Some Americans argue that we are the wealthiest nation because we are more intelligent, more virtuous, and more industrious. This, too, is hardly true to the facts nor fair to the other peoples of the world.

What, then, is the explanation? The Christian sees this affluence as a gift of God's providence. The nation was born at an opportune time. It was protected by two mighty oceans. It was not encumbered with European traditions. It was blessed with fantastic resources and a fascinating mixture of people, who in their very diversity of origin and race released tremendous energy into the development of the land, the factories, and the culture. If we *do* see our wealth as a gift of providence, we are prepared psychologically to share it as belonging to God and not to ourselves. That is all that is asked by churches outside the United States. In the years ahead the opportunity to use our abundance both as national and church policy looms before us as a test of our understanding of stewardship. The potential giving for a missionary outreach in the United States and throughout the world is far beyond anything we have done.

Sacrifice

Men and women sent to the critical "no-man's land" between faith and unbelief will learn immediately one lesson. They will go with no other power than that which comes from their religious faith. The color of their skin, the use of English, the administrative

145

skills they have acquired will be no automatic passport to success. Their problem is to offer themselves as servants without power, and this is not easy. This is also the test of the pastor in the local congregation who begins to see himself as one who teaches laymen to be missionaries rather than being himself the center. For Americans this is painful, but it is the challenge of the day. The same is true for American churches as they see their financial resources being used overseas. Dealing with the younger churches as brothers means sharing with them a gift and not insisting on control of it.

The Younger Churches Regroup

In the last century the relationship of older and younger churches was that of parent and child. In this century we have seen it has become that of brother and brother. We need to see one further development in the relationship between the older and younger churches. This is the regrouping of the younger churches. For example, the major Protestant churches in the seventeen countries of Asia, beginning with Pakistan and running around the rim of China all the way to Japan, have come together in the East Asia Christian Conference. The same development has taken place in Africa and Latin America. Many in the Western world still feel that interdenominational missionary planning is the task of the Western churches. But this is no longer true. The East Asia Christian Conference, which includes the major denominations in Asia, sees its task as that of providing a forum where Asian churches can by themselves think through the next steps in fulfilling the unfinished task of mission in Asia. Their future agendas include a cluster of other problems. One is the role of confessional churches such as the Lutheran, Episcopal, and Methodist churches in Asia. They are asking if this is the right direction for the future.

A second question concerns the relationship of the churches in Asia and their parent bodies in the United States and Europe. Should these relationships be unilateral as they have been in the past? Or should the major denominations in the United States be encouraged to have multilateral relationships with other denominations in Asia?

A third question deals with the problems of theological education, Christian literature, Christian colleges and high schools, Christian hospitals, and mass communication such as radio and television. Should this coordination be provided by Western mis-

146

sionary bodies, or should missionary programs of this kind be interdenominational and directed from centers in Asia, Africa, and Latin America?

Relationships with the Roman Catholic Church

The Roman Catholic Church realizes, as do the Protestant churches, the seriousness of the present world situation. There is a new openness of mind and spirit. There are more and more meetings of theologians discussing the issues of faith. There were five Roman Catholic observers at the New Delhi meeting of the World Council of Churches in 1961. Pope John calls Protestants "the separated brethren." There will be representatives of the Protestant churches attending the Vatican Council in 1963 called by Pope John XXIII. It would be unrealistic to expect any serious movement toward reunion at this time. If it comes, it will be decades away and only after God has overruled objections on both sides. The deep Protestant fear of Roman Catholic power remains. However, we may see a growing Bible study, theological discussion, more and more contacts between laymen, more intercessory prayer on both sides, and some experiments in working together to meet emergency situations of human suffering. There is an element of risk when we think of discussions of this kind. But we live in such an age, and God seems to be preparing all those who name the name of Christ in any way for some kind of reconciliation in spirit.

The following sentence is like a child's riddle, but there is truth in it.

The sentence goes, "Protestants and Roman Catholics *disagree* in the faith; but they disagree *in the faith*."

Beyond Liberalism and Fundamentalism

There is genuine hope that there will be growing contacts with the more conservative groups. Some of the lines that have separated Protestants are disappearing. One cannot underestimate the missionary outreach of these groups into the nation and into the world. Already 62 per cent of North American missionaries represent these churches. The evangelist Billy Graham appears to have helped bridge the gulf between these segments within Protestantism. Here again the difficulties are many. The non-historical churches will feel the risks of working together more than the

147

mainline churches. Yet if one of the genuine points of Protestant understanding of the Church is that of an instrument or earthen vessel that is to be constantly reformed, then neither side should be afraid of change.

To Sum Up

As we look back over the past fifty years, we can see that the Protestant churches have been experiencing what would appear to be a sustained effort to understand each other and to plan together for the future. Their meetings have been frequent, and always the agenda has been the same. What are the signs of the time, they have asked, and what is God saying to us through the Scripture regarding his mission to the world? It has been a period of questioning and uncertainty. Yet through it all the signs are unmistakable. The churches are coming together; the visible signs are seen in their willingness to witness to each other, to work together, and to wait in readiness as to what God wills for the future. No one can predict what this will mean. But one thing is clear. The churches are being drawn together for a purpose. The Christian is bold enough to say that the purpose is preparation for an intensified missionary effort now under way, and which will extend into the century ahead.

A Postscript
On Hope

"Peace to all of you who are in Christ" (I Peter 4:14).

MARTIN LUTHER wrote that Christians are merry men of God who are merry when there is nothing to be merry about. The more one thinks over these words, the more important they become as an understanding of Christian hope. Luther's words are a reminder that the source of a Christian's hope comes not from within but from beyond the world. Joyous, radiant hope in the future is meaningful only if it is based on what God from a world beyond has done and will do. It does not follow from this that we can see no signs of hope in the present. There *are* such signs. We can see them even in those parts of the world where the Church is a minority and under attack.

Such a picture comes into focus as we look at the Christian Church in Communist China. In no one place in the contemporary world has the mission of the Church been harder hit. If we can see the sources of hope for Christians in China, we should be able to feel hope for the Church anywhere in the world.

We have seen in an earlier chapter that Christians in China have lived in the electric, restless, angry, and confused atmosphere of Communist revolution. This revolution has been one of struggle and hardship. Through it all Christians have been humbled, frightened, humiliated, isolated, and manipulated. Yet they have survived. No one remains a Christian in China today for personal gain. Christian students find it harder to get into the university. Christian graduates find it more difficult to get good jobs. Christian ministers are subject to the charge that they are agents of Western imperialism or spies of the United States. One thing is certain: the Christian fence-sitters are gone. Those who openly call themselves Christians do so because they believe what they say about Christ. As we look at the future of the Christian Church in China, what can we learn? What does an appraisal of its experience teach us about hope?

149

Faith in the Stubbornness of the Church

There are five acts in the long drama of winning the Chinese to Jesus Christ.[1]

The first act began in A.D. 635 when the Nestorian missionaries arrived. At first they were well received. For almost 200 years they survived. Then in 845 a serious persecution broke out. In the year 900, an Arab visiting China learned from the Emperor that he knew about Noah, the prophets, Moses, and Jesus, and even had portraits of them. But by 987 there was no trace left of this knowledge. The first act ended in failure.

The second act began in the 13th century. In 1294 a priest named John of Montecorvino visited Peking. John and his fellow missionaries built churches in and around Peking. Seventy-four years later, in 1368, when the Mongol dynasty collapsed, the new rulers, the Mings, turned on the Christians. Every sign of Christian influence was ruthlessly stamped out. Three hundred years later when missionaries again entered China, a few of them claimed either to have seen or heard of families that crossed themselves before eating, but when asked why they did so, they did not know. The second act, like the first was a failure.

The third act curtain went up in 1552, when Francis Xavier, the Jesuit missionary, visited the island of Macao. He tried to enter China, but was refused. He died waiting for the opportunity. The very year that he died, a child was born in Europe named Mathew Ricci. Ricci's career as a Jesuit missionary to the Chinese was amazing. He wore only Chinese dress, changed his name to that of a Chinese, became a recognized scholar in the Chinese classics, and introduced the Chinese to the modern calendar. He made such an impression on the Emperor that he was assigned a special house and was supported by imperial funds. In spite of this early success, in the years that followed it appeared again and again that the Church would be crushed by periodic persecutions. In each period of testing the number of Christians would drop, but once the crisis was over the churches continued to grow.

The fourth act was played throughout the 19th century. In the year 1807, at the age of 25, Robert Morrison arrived in Canton. He faced every discouragement and obstacle. It was seven years after he began his work before he baptized his first convert. After 25

[1] Cary-Elwes, *China and the Cross*. This thought is developed throughout the book.

years, only ten had been baptized. During the next 150 years the Church saw tremendous advance. The Christian gospel, along with democratic ideas, revolutionized Chinese civilization. In this period literally hundreds of schools, hospitals, and other forms of social service were opened. The churches grew in number and strength of leadership. This fourth act came to an end in 1949 when the Communists swept over China.

We are now witnessing the fifth act. Christians in China are numerically weak. They have been and are being harassed, but they have survived. Hope is reborn when we see the five-act drama of the church, reaching back many centuries. We see here a stubbornness about Christian faith. We need this perspective as we look at the world in which we live. We turn to the past not only to learn from our mistakes but also to find courage and hope as we look at the future.

Faith Means We Trust Fellow Christians

To live by hope means that we trust fellow Christians. We must trust them even if they disagree with us politically. This is true of our relationship with Christians in China. They support the Communist government. They have no other alternative. Furthermore, some of them genuinely believe that the present government is the best one China has had. We disagree, but that should not separate us from them or shatter our trust in them as Christians. It is never easy to put into practice the Christian teaching that a common loyalty to Jesus Christ is more binding between two people than loyalty to one's nation, class, or race. Yet this is the test of faith. Nowhere is this more evident than in our dealings with Christians in China. If we could be confident of their integrity and their loyalty to Christ, we would see immediately that the same trust is possible in our relationship to Christians in Africa and Latin America, not to mention Russia and Poland. When this trust becomes a reality, we see Christians quietly but powerfully holding the world together.

Love Is Stronger Than Hate

No American suffered more at the hands of the Communists than the Methodist missionary Gertrude Cone. The *Manchester Guardian* of March 14, 1952, reported her arrival in Hong Kong:

151

A report from Hong Kong describes a cold-blooded atrocity by the Chinese communists. In the town of Nanchang, a Methodist woman missionary, Gertrude Cone, had been suffering from cancer. She was not allowed in the hospital. She slowly starved. When at last it came to the notice of the authorities that she was near death, they arranged transport to Hong Kong with a doctor and nurse, who gave her injections to keep her going until she was over the frontier. She died two days later, and the hospital authorities stated that she was the worst malnutrition case which they had ever seen.

When her stretcher was carried by the Communists to the dividing no-man's land between Hong Kong and Communist China, it was placed on the ground. The Communist doctor and nurse checked her again to be sure she would live to cross the line. During the trip they had shown no friendliness to her. A day later before she died, she told Bishop Ralph Ward, "I couldn't preach; I couldn't talk to people, but I could pray for them. So I never ceased to pray for my friends. I have no hatred in my heart toward anyone." She told of the stop on the border when the Communist doctor examined her. She said, "I thanked him from the bottom of my heart for his care; and when I did, he looked very embarrassed."

Missionary Responsibility Cannot Be Forfeited

It is important for Christians of all lands to be concerned about the Chinese. So far as the present is concerned, the major missionary task falls on the Christians who live in China itself. There will be no mission in China at all unless Christians there perform it. Having said this, I maintain that Christians *outside* China cannot forfeit their responsibility to the Chinese. This means that Japanese, Indonesian, German, Congolese, Brazilian, as well as American Christians must see the Chinese as their responsibility. The missionary task of Christians can never be forfeited to only those living within any one nation.

Bishop Ralph A. Ward recognized this. Having spent many years in China, he was forced to leave by the Communists. However, up to his 76th year he continued to help and train Chinese wherever he could find them. In Hong Kong shortly before his death in 1958 he ordained three young Chinese men. They knelt at his bedside. Bishop Ward was so weak that his voice was barely audible. Only with help could he sit up in bed. After placing his hands on the heads of the young men and ordaining them, he said to them in Chinese, "Go preach! Go preach!" It is a statement of fact that within a few moments he fell into a coma from which he never recovered. His last words are a reminder to every non-Chinese Christian of what God requires of his disciples. Every Christian is responsible for the people of other races and nations. Asian and African Christians cannot forfeit their responsibility to witness to Americans. Our spiritual lives are their concern. They are as responsible to proclaim the Gospel to us as we are to proclaim it to them. This mutuality and interdependence of Christians is one of the most hopeful factors to be seen within the world today.

The Expectation That Something Is Going to Happen

Many threatening signs surround us. There is the danger of war. There is the threat of revolution. In spite of this, Christians are to live always in the expectation that something marvelous is going to take place. There are signs that this is happening. We can see it in the world of science and technology. A new day of opportunity has dawned. Technological development is not against God. In itself it is neither good nor bad; its effect depends entirely on how man uses it. There is every reason to hope that mankind will develop the political structures necessary to make possible man's survival. For this Christians must both hope and work.

We can also expect something to happen to the Church. In fact, it *is* happening. Even against its will it is being reformed, remade. What will be its form fifty or a hundred years from now we cannot say.

We can expect something to happen to ourselves. Our old way of life can be transformed into lives that have both purity and joy. We can also expect something to happen to the world at large. We can believe that 500 years from now historians will declare that during the 19th and 20th centuries the most creative movement among the Chinese was not the rise of Communism but the spreading and deepening of the roots of Christian faith into the culture, the mind, and the life of the Chinese people. We know that this will not come without suffering. But if it is possible in China, it is possible in every other part of the world. "And he who sat upon the throne said, 'Behold, I make all things

153

new'" (Rev. 21:5). It has been true in the past; it remains true today.

Dependence on God

It is always precarious to draw too sharp a distinction between missionary eras. There *are* distinctions, to be sure. The missionary ideas of the 19th century are changing; a new understanding is growing. Yet both the old and the new are rooted in God's act of reconciliation. Paul's missionary life and those of David Livingstone and Francis Asbury are understandable only in terms of their dependence upon God. The same is true of our lives. Fifty years from now our children's children will look back on the period through which we are passing and wonder why we could not see more clearly the meaning of our time. As were Livingstone and Asbury, we are being swept along by the stream of history. Try as we do, we cannot leap high enough out of the water to see further than the next bend. We cannot know whether there are cataracts or quieter waters ahead. One thing we *do* know.

The river will continue to flow at an even faster pace and the mystery of man's existence will continue to surround him. Thus we end this book where its introduction began: with our eyes on Jesus Christ. He alone illumines for us the redemptive purposes of God. It is in his cross that we see the love and the power of God coming together. This remains for us a mystery. But when we live by it, it provides not only meaning for our lives but also power to do that which otherwise we are incapable of doing.

When David Livingstone was buried in Westminster Abbey, his favorite hymn was sung:

> "O God of Bethel, by whose hand
> Thy people still are fed. . . ." [2]

The last verse of the hymn ends seeking God's presence "till all our wanderings cease." Remembering David Livingstone's life of constant travel, one can see why this hymn meant so much to him. The age in which we live has changed. The missionary situation is a far cry from what it was. But God's sovereign purpose that all mankind shall find wholeness and meaning to their lives

---

[2] Fosdick, *Dear Mr. Brown*, p. 94.

is as real as when Livingstone was mauled by a lion, buried his wife in the jungle, and died on his knees by a cot. The God who was with him is with us. He is the living God working today in this fascinating, threatening world. With Christians throughout the world we are called on as individuals to be co-workers with him. So was Paul called. So was Livingstone called. In an emerging world civilization we must point by our words and our lives to Jesus Christ, whom God has lifted up and made the cornerstone of the age to come.

Index

Anonymity 89-90
Andrews, C. F. 87
Anxiety 69 f.
Asbury, Francis 18-9, 28, 107, 154
Automation 135-6

Batchelder, R. C. 31
Barbarian 25
Barth, K. 60
Bennett, J. C. 72
Berdyaev, N. 72
Black, E. R. 35
Bonhoeffer, D. 68
Booth, A. 134
Brunner, E. 86
Buddhism 12, 19, 36, 39, 57, 60, 70, 88, 108, 122-3
Butler, S. 45

Camus, A. 118
Carey, William 18-9
Cartwright, Peter 23, 28
Cary-Elwes, Columba 18, 150
Charles, P. 59
Chen, W. Y. 50
China 8, 35, 150 (see "Communism")
—missionaries 150 ff.
Chou, Ivy 125
Christ (see Jesus)
Christians:
—and Jews 97
—and nation-state 128 ff.
—distinctiveness of 88-9
—laymen 113-4
—population 112
—trust among 151
Church:
—and nations 132-3
—as conscience 128 ff.
—as minority 116
—as servant 127-37
—as summons 83 ff.
—continuity 63-4
—in Communist China 48-53
—mission to 114-5

—stubbornness 150-1
—world-wide 12, 29, 111
—younger 143, 146-7
Churchill, Winston 28
Circuit riders 27
Cleveland, H. 114
Communism 11, 19, 36, 39, 88, 89
—China 48-53, 57, 89, 95, 123-4, 151-3
Community 63
—inclusive 86
Compassion 62
Cone, Gertrude 151-2
Conquest 101-2
Conscience, church as 128 ff.
Continuity 63
Cousins, N. 37
Cragg, K. 120

Death 102-3, 123
Decisions, complex 46-8
Denominationalism 142
Dickson, M. 125
Discipline 87
Dread 70

Earthquake 41 f.
Economic 26
Ecumenical movement 12, 29, 111-2, 139-48
Einstein, A. 31
Expectation 153-5
Explorers 26-9, 139-48

Faith 69 ff.
Famine 101
Ferry, W. H. 136
Fifth Horseman 103
Forsyth, P. T. 45, 64
Fosdick, H. E. 137, 154
Four Horsemen 101-3
Freedom 65-7
Frustration 71
Fundamentalism 147

Galbraith, J. K. 7, 132
God
—as missionary 57, 60, 64-5

—dependence on 154-5
—kingdom of 93 ff.
—sovereignty 66-7
Great Commission 62
Greek view 25

Hamilton, W. 7, 110
Heathen 25
Herberg, W. 99
Hinduism 12, 20, 36, 39, 57, 60, 71, 108, 121-2
History 101
Holy Spirit 65-7
Hope 149-55
Hudson, W. S. 44, 141
Humanity, new 83
—misery of 137
Independence:
—new nations 11
Islam 12, 36, 57, 60, 71, 88, 119-21

Jesus Christ 13, 21, 40, 65, 69, 73, 80-1, 86, 93-6, 103, 108, 112, 117, 121 ff., 128, 131, 154-5
—finality of 80
—hidden 72
Jews, mission to 96-100
Joy 90
Judson, Adoniram 25

Kafka, F. 71
Kierkegaard, S. 85
Kingdom of God 93 ff.
Kraemer, H. 39, 60, 116

Lacy, C. 50
Latourette, K. S. 19, 64
Laymen 113-4, 141
Lester, M. 49-50
Liberalism 147
Liberator 23-6, 127-37
Livingstone, David 20-9, 107, 127, 154-5
Love 67
Luther, M. 124, 131, 139, 149

157

INDEX

MacInnis, F. 125
MacKenzie, K. M. 25-6
MacLeod, G. F. 130
Malaya 61 f.
Man, condition of 75-6
Mangone, G. J. 114
Marty, M. E. 45, 134
Marxists 118-9
Materialists 117-8
Mathews, J. K. 120
Methodists 141
Missiles 37
Mission field 21, 107 ff.
Missionary:
—China 150
—critics 9
—era ends 17
—foreign 141
—God 57 ff.
—motives 58, 62-4, 69 f.
—responsibility 152-3
—success 144
—wisdom 22, 113-26, 139-48
—who is? 114
Missions:
—Protestant 17
Motives:
—for unity 141-2
—missionary 58, 62-4, 69 f.
Muslims (see Islam)
Myers, C. K. 79-80, 133-4

National missions 134-5, 140
Nationalism 35-6, 128 f.
Nation-state 128, 140

Neill, S. 43, 96-7
New age, beginning of 9-14
—technological 33
—unexpected 32
Niebuhr, H. R. 23
Niebuhr, R. 72, 98
Nietzsche 43
Niles, D. T. 63, 123
No-man's land 107 ff.
Nuclear power 36-7

Paul 74, 86, 87, 88, 98, 155
Perry, E. 119-20
Population explosion 35, 116, 140
Power 67
Privacy 88-9
Project Apollo 10
Protestants 44-5, 59, 107-8

Race 133-4
Revolution 34-5, 37
—theological 59-60
Roman Catholicism 13, 17, 44, 59, 63, 142, 147
Roman heritage 25

Sacrifice 145
Secularism 13
Self-confidence, loss of 45-6
Shinn, R. L. 94
Silone, Ignazio 110
Spike, R. W. 135-6
Stewardship 145

Stewart, J. S. 42, 62
Sweetman, J. W. 59

Technology 10, 33-4, 36-8
Theological:
—erosion 42-3
—revolution 59-60
Tolerance 89
Toynbee, A. 39, 67-8

United Nations 47, 112
Urban work 134-5

Varg, P. A. 25
Vatican Council 147
Visser 't Hooft, W. A. 139

Wang Ming Tao 50-1
War 102
Ward, Ralph 152-3
Warren, M. A. C. 84
Webber, G. W. 60-1, 135
Werner, H. G. 86
Wesley, John 17-8, 141
West, decline of 10-11
Whitehead, A. N. 44
Williams, D. D. 23
Witness 69 ff., 143
World:
—church 111-2 (see ecumenical movement)
—civilization 31 ff., 38-9
—religions 116
—technology 36-8
World Council of Churches 127, 139-41, 147

OUR MISSION TODAY

The

Beginning of a

New Age

Tracey K. Jones, Jr.

World Outlook Press
475 Riverside Drive
New York 27, New York

5th Printing
185th Thousand

Library of Congress Catalog Number 63-10784

Set in 11 pt. and 10 pt. Granjon, printed and bound by The Parthenon Press, Nashville, Tennessee

SB85-MPH-10-63-30M